Gospelsongfully Yours
P. P. Bliss.

Page 139.

Ira D. Sankey

Page 129.

SONG VICTORIES

OF

"THE BLISS AND SANKEY HYMNS,"

BEING A COLLECTION OF ONE HUNDRED INCIDENTS IN REGARD TO THE ORIGIN AND POWER OF THE HYMNS CONTAINED IN "GOSPEL HYMNS AND SACRED SONGS."

WITH AN INTRODUCTORY LETTER

BY REV. GEO. F. PENTECOST, D.D.

AND AN APPENDIX

CONTAINING BIOGRAPHICAL SKETCHES OF

MR. IRA D. SANKEY AND MR. P. P. BLISS.

Boston:

Published by D. Lothrop & Co.

Dover, N. H.: G. T. Day & Co.

TO

THE SINGING EVANGELISTS,

THIS LITTLE BOOK
IS DEDICATED, WITH THE PRAYER THAT
IT MAY LEAD OTHERS TO

SING THE GOSPEL.

CONTENTS.

PAGE

INTRODUCTORY LETTER. 7

[*What a Pastor has Felt and Seen of the Power of Sacred Song.*]

THE POWER OF SONG UPON CHILDHOOD. 8

POWER OF SONG IN YOUNG MANHOOD. 9

SONG AS A DELIVERER. 11

SONG AS A HELP TO CONSECRATION. 15

SONG AS A MEANS OF CONVERSION. 17

HYMNS IN PUBLIC WORSHIP. 19

HYMNS IN THE PRAYER-MEETING. 20

THE POWER OF SONG IN THE REVIVAL WORK OF MOODY AND SANKEY. 21

HYMN INCIDENTS, ... 31

CONSECRATED VOICES. 125

APPENDIX. 129

Biographical Sketch of Mr. I. D. Sankey. 129

Biographical Sketch of Mr. P. P. Bliss. 139

ALPHABETICAL INDEX

OF

HYMN INCIDENTS.

	PAGE
Almost persuaded, ...	115
All hail the power of Jesus' name, ...	91
Arise, my soul, arise, ...	118
Brightly beams our Father's mercy, ...	48
Come home! come home!	46
Come thou Fount of every blessing, ...	119
Depths of mercy! can there be, ...	108
Free from the law, oh happy condition, ...	112
Guide me, O thou Great Jehovah, ...	112
Have you on the Lord believed?	106
Hold the fort, ...	47
I am coming to the cross, ...	51
I am so glad that our Father in heaven, ...	31

PAGE

I gave my life for thee, ... 60
I hear the Saviour say, ... 43
In the Christian's home in glory, ... 55

Jesus, lover of my soul, ... 62
Just as I am without one plea, ... 120

Light in the darkness, sailor, ... 50
Lord, I hear of showers of blessing, ... 57

My faith looks up to Thee, ... 102

Nearer, my God, to Thee, ... 100

O for a thousand tongues to sing, ... 98
Only an armor-bearer, ... 51

Praise God, from whom all blessings flow, ... 122

Ring the bells of heaven, ... 53
Rock of Ages, cleft for me, ... 86

Safe in the arms of Jesus, ... 58
Sowing the seed by the daylight fair, ... 37
Stand up, stand up for Jesus, ... 119

There is a fountain filled with blood, ... 93
There is a gate that stands ajar, ... 43

PAGE

There is a land of pure delight, ... 116

There were ninety and nine, ... 107

To-day the Saviour calls, ... 60

What means this eager, anxious throng? 40

Yet there is room! the Lamb's bright hall of song, . 45

INTRODUCTORY LETTER.

"SING ye praises with the understanding."

"Our days of praise shall ne'er be past
While life and thought and being last,
Or immortality endures."

I have fancied sometimes the Bethel-bent beam
That trembled to earth in the Patriarch's dream,
Was a ladder of song in that wilderness rest
From the pillow of stone to the blue of the Blest,
And the angels descending to dwell with us here,
"Old Hundred," and "Corinth," and "China," and "Mear."

WHAT A PASTOR HAS FELT AND SEEN OF THE POWER OF SACRED SONG.

BY REV. GEO. F. PENTECOST, OF BOSTON.

My Dear Brother:

YOU ask me to give you, from my own personal experience and observation, any facts in relation to the use and power of sacred song in connection with the work of the Holy Spirit for the conversion and sanctification of sinners; and I most gladly bear my testimony.

I presume my experience is not different in kind from that of all other Christians who have submitted themselves to God under this wonderful instrument of the Spirit.

THE POWER OF SONG UPON CHILDHOOD.

Some of my earliest religious awakenings were in connection with the hymns for children that were just beginning to be sung in the Sabbath-schools when I was yet a little boy. I mention one beginning:

"I think when I read that sweet story of old,
When Jesus was here among men,
How He called little children like lambs to His fold:
I should like to have been with them then."

That little hymn would always quiet me and beget within my heart seriousness and longing. When as a child I used to hear or sing it, I would wonder if there was any blessing that I might have from Jesus that would correspond to His calling little children to Him, and laying His gentle, loving hands on their heads and blessing them. And in after years, when I had grown to be a young man, away from home, and far from God by wicked works, that little hymn of my childhood would often come to my memory; and more than once I have sung it with choking voice and tearful eye, and with motions of real penitence in my heart. It is true that these effects were transient, but they were real and mighty; and I doubt not that God used that child's hymn and the sweet echoes of many others — now forgotten — to keep my heart from becoming perfectly hardened against His "gentle voice."

POWER OF SONG IN YOUNG MANHOOD.

To-day, on looking back over the fourteen years that have passed since I gave my life to Jesus, among the precious recollections of those happy days I recall a few dear old hymns that sung themselves into my heart, and taught me truths of God that otherwise I might not have learned, and led me to the sources of joy and delight which otherwise I might not have found. I can hear those voices now, that used to lead the singing in that blessed revival time. Some of them, it is true, were poor and cracked and discordant—it was a congregation of "common people"—and would have utterly spoiled and ruined any songs other than those of the sanctuary, that were sung in those hours of the Spirit's presence and power, with hearts making melody to the Lord. I think it was the singing of that simple old hymn and chorus—which I now quote—that awakened in me the desire to be a Christian, by setting before me its promise of "sweetest pleasure" and "solid comfort" in strong contrast with the unsatisfying portions I was getting from worldly pleasures, and the fear and dread of death that was so constantly before me:—

"'Tis religion that can give,
In the light, in the light,
Sweetest pleasure while we live;
In the light of God.

'Tis religion must supply,
In the light, in the light,
Solid comfort when we die,
In the light of God.

Let us walk in the light,
In the light, in the light,
Let us walk in the light,
In the light of God."

Eternity only will reveal the power that hymn had over me, both in bringing me to God, and in strengthening and encouraging me in the first days of trial and temptation that came to me as a young Christian.

Time would fail me to speak at length of my experimental relations to those old classics,—

"There is a fountain filled with blood,"
"Rock of ages, cleft for me,"
"Jesus, lover of my soul," &c.

SONG AS A DELIVERER.

I am profoundly sure that among the divinely ordained instrumentalities for the conversion and sanctification of the soul, God has not given a greater, beside the preaching of the gospel, than the singing of "psalms and hymns and spiritual songs." I have known a hymn to do God's work in a soul when every other instrumentality has failed. I could not enumerate the times God has rescued and saved my soul from darkness, discouragement, and weariness, by the singing of a hymn, generally by bringing one to my own heart and causing me to sing it to myself.

A year or two after I entered the ministry, I passed through an experience that on the dark side of it culminated in leading me to believe not only that I had been mistaken in supposing that God had called me to the work of the ministry, but also that I was even mistaken in supposing that I was a Christian at all. Oh! the blackness and darkness of those hours! I cannot portray the dense gloom that gathered about my soul, and was fairly pressing me down to hell. In this fearful state of mind, having almost yielded up to despair, I was returning to my home from a neighboring town where I had been assisting(?) a "ministering brother" in a "protracted meeting." I got aboard the train, flung myself into a seat next a window of the car, and made another desperate effort to recover myself, my faith, my hope, my confidence in God. I prayed in Spirit,

I even called aloud on God, unmindful of the people around me; I went over the promises, and searched my memory through for some word of the Lord that would bring me help. But God's Word was a silent and sealed book for me, and my heart seemed to be turning into stone. In the midst of this wretchedness I was looking out of the car window up into the star-lit heavens, and wondering if there was a God, if there was any Jesus, any Christ, if there was any hereafter. While thus gazing into the dimly lighted darkness without, from out of the midnight darkness within, with only the numb sense of my own wretchedness, as a man might feel who knows he is freezing to death without power to help himself, and, indeed, not caring to any longer, because it seems easier to die, I heard the low voice of singing in my heart, *I say I heard the voice of singing within me*, and harkening I caught the words of it, and with my own lips in low, tremulous tones began to sing,—

"Jesus, I my cross have taken,
All to leave and follow Thee:
Naked, poor, despised, forsaken,
Thou from hence my all shall be."

I wondered at myself and at the song—I found my heart softening—I knew that tears were in my eyes—I felt them running down my cheeks—I was away back with Jesus on the cross—I heard his cry, "My God! My God! why hast thou forsaken me?" and in that same moment the Holy Ghost gave me fellowship with my Saviour, and I knew that cry from him was not for himself alone, but for *me*. I sang on through the hymn with still melting heart, with returning faith, hope and confidence, until in a perfect ecstacy of peace I reached the lines,—

> "Oh, 'tis not in griefs to harm me,
> While Thy love is left to me;
> Oh! 'twere not in joy to charm me,
> Were that joy unmixed with Thee."

And then, like a comforted child, I fairly laid my weary heart against His dear loving heart, knowing in my soul that *He loved me*, that He *died* and *rose* again for me, that He lived for me and that as never before *we* were united to *each other*. Thus that precious hymn was God's hand reached out to save me when I was sinking; thus He was pleased to manifest

Himself to me in a sweeter, surer, and stronger way than I had yet known him. He had chosen to do this by and in a hymn, rather than by prayer, or meditation, or promise. As the cake baked on the coals and the cruse of water at his head were to Elijah, so was that hymn to me; at least it was the hand of the angel that touched me and pointed me to the "true bread" and the "living water" in the strength of which, having eaten and drank, I went many days, yea, and am still even now walking.

SONG AS A HELP TO CONSECRATION.

Years after when I was passing through consecration into deeper fellowship with the Lord, it pleased him to use that same hymn again; this time not so much for immediate *comfort* as for *searching*. By inward teaching the Spirit was making me to know something of the meaning of the Master when he said, "If any man will come after me let him deny *himself*, and take up *his* cross daily and follow *me*." Whilst I was learning somewhat painfully this lesson, I was one day suddenly checked in the singing of this, one of my favorite hymns, with the distinct question, "can you *truly* sing,—

> 'Jesus, *I my* cross have *taken,*
> *All* to leave and follow *Thee?*'"

I say I found myself checked in the singing of it for a long time; until, in my deepest heart and purpose, I had truly denied myself into his hands, to be "armed with the same mind." But now, "thanks be unto God who always giveth us the victory," after having been searched by it, as I was never searched before, I can joyfully and honestly sing that doubly dear old hymn "in the Spirit and with the understanding also." The Lord always makes it a great comfort and power to my soul. And as a response to that hymn, now, always come those lines of Charles Wesley's great psalm,—

> "Thou, *O Christ,* art *all* I want,
> More than all in *Thee* I find."

I might magnify the grace of God ministered to me, by reference to many more hymns, but as the above may serve for illustrations of the use God has made of hymns in deal ing with my own soul, I pass to record, in a similar manner, the power of song as I have witnessed it in others, coming under my own pastoral care.

SONG AS A MEANS OF CONVERSION.

I said above that I have known a hymn to be used of God for the conversion of a soul where every other means had failed to bring light into the darkened and troubled heart. Once I was detained after prayer-meeting with a few others, to converse and pray with a young woman who was under deep conviction, and who refused to go away from the place of prayer until she had found Jesus. It seemed to be all in vain that I talked with her, explaining the atonement, quoting the simplest and strongest promises of the gospel, and urging her to an immediate and simple faith; it was all in vain that I prayed with and for her. At last, because — as it seemed — I could do nothing else, I began to sing that little hymn, the last verse of which goes,—

"Oh! bear my longing heart to Him
Who bled and died for me;

Whose blood now cleanses from all sin,
And gives me victory."

We had sung the whole hymn through, and were hushed into silence by the Spirit. During the singing of the last stanza, our friend had lifted her weeping face toward mine, and was looking intently and eagerly at me, as though she would fain drink in the words and power of the song. And now in the hush that was upon us, reaching out both her hands to me, she said, in a plaintive kind of whisper,—

"Please sing that last verse again."

And again we sang, softly and tenderly,—

"Oh! bear my longing soul to Him
Who bled and died for me;
Whose blood now cleanses from all sin,
And gives me victory."

As the words and melody died away, the expression of her face changed; the darkness was overpast, and the light and gladness of His peace had come in the place of it; and with a cry of joy she turned and flung herself into the arms of her sister, who was standing near, exclaiming, "I am saved! I am saved!! Oh! blessed Jesus," &c.

Incidents of this kind might be multiplied, but this one may suffice to illustrate the power of song in the conversion of souls to God.

HYMNS IN PUBLIC WORSHIP.

It would be easy to fill many pages with interesting facts in connection with the use of hymns in the public worship of the house of God. I have seen vast audiences melted and swayed by a simple hymn when they have been unmoved by a powerful presentation of the gospel from the pulpit. From close and repeated observation, I am persuaded that Mr. Spurgeon, the great metropolitan preacher of England, places great reliance on the use of his hymns in public worship. By them he prepares his vast audiences for the service that is to follow; and fastens his discourse with a hymn, which he always reads with great power, and which is sung by that vast choir of 7500 people with an effect that is indescribable. Indeed, the use of hymns in the service of the sanctuary, when in the hands of a pastor or leader who understands and feels the inspiration of them, cannot be too highly estimated. It is a great pity that the power of "psalms and hymns and spiritual songs" has been so sadly weakened, if not utterly destroyed by the introduction of "fancy quartettes," who sing neither with the "spirit nor with the understanding," and who practically forbid any one else to sing. Lord, hasten the day when the service of song shall be restored to the people.

IN THE PRAYER-MEETING

Hymns are simply indispensable. A pastor *skilled in the use* of them holds the prayer-meeting almost absolutely in his power. An unfortunate or ill-timed address or exhortation may be covered by a hymn, and the people's hearts and minds brought back to God. A pungent address, a ringing testimony, or a prevaling prayer may be strongly supplemented and reinforced by a well chosen hymn promptly and sweetly sung, which, without giving out page or number, shall have sprung spontaneously from the lips of the pastor or *any* brother or sister in the congregation who has spiritual discernment. For myself I should feel utterly lost, and without "sword" or "trowel" for the building and defence of the walls of Zion, if I were without the "armory" and "kit" of hymns which God has given the church "to profit withal."

THE POWER OF SONG IN THE REVIVAL WORK OF MOODY AND SANKEY.

I shall close this letter by giving a brief account of the triumph of song as seen in connection with the great revival of the last few years on both sides of the Atlantic. All know the story of the "two" simple-hearted and "unlearned" men — Moody and Sankey — who went only a few years ago, "led of the spirit," to the British Isles, to preach and *sing* the gospel "there also." Moody with his open Bible, Sankey with his budget of stirring hymns, and his sweet God-given and sanctified voice. It is exceedingly doubtful from all the testimony I could gather which had the most to do in the awakening and stirring which Scotland and Ireland have received at their hands. Whether most is to be ascribed to Moody's preaching, or a Sankey's singing — one with simple words of truth, the other with sweetest song — represent a two-edged instrument which the Holy Spirit has been pleased to use in the accomplishment of this mighty work. But certain it is that whoever visits Scotland for years to come will know that *Sankey* has been there, for he has sung a hundred sweet songs into the hearts and spiritual lives of more than *twenty thousand* converts to Jesus, and has filled the whole land, Highlands and Lowlands, with their sacred echoes.

Eminent Scotch clergymen told me, while in conversation with them on this subject, that it was Sankey's singing that melted the hearts of the people and made an open door for Moody with his Bible lessons, for such they were rather than sermons. Of course this is not mentioned to disparage the *preaching* of the gospel — God forbid — but only to show the relation of song to the spoken word. This service of song in Scotland was not a passing gift — it is a permanent legacy. None may reproduce Moody's matchless Bible expositions, but all Scotland for years to come will sing Sankey's songs.

It was in the Barkley church in Edinburgh where these apostles of the Word and song began their work, having been invited thither by the noble pastor, Rev. James Wilson, who was an advanced advocate of "*hymns and spiritual songs*," as well as "*psalms*." I was in that church, the guest of the pastor, during a crowded Thursday evening prayer-meeting. In deference to the time-honored custom of the Scotch, Mr. Wilson gave out a paraphrase of one of David's psalms. The congregation did bravely and well, considering the meter and the melody (?). But after the meeting was formally opened, the book of Paraphrases was quietly tucked under the pulpit and one of our little American hymns announced: —

'I hear thy gentle voice,
  That calls me, Lord, to thee;
For cleansing in the precious blood
  That flowed on Calvary."

In a twinkling every one present whipped out of pocket a little penny copy of "Sankey's Hymns;" every face was radiant, and every voice was vocal. The house seemed filled with the Spirit, and every heart seemed to be pouring out its faith and hope to God in the hymn that had in all probability led many of those present to Christ, and had quickened the faith and hope of all. I hope the Paraphrases will not be given up, and I am sure they will not; but they will be improved, some of them, and sung all the better for the baptism that they are being baptized with — how are they straitened until it be accomplished. I witnessed the same effect in Dr. Wallace's great congregation in Glasgow, the same in Dr. Bonar's church, the same in the great noonday meetings in Assembly Hall, and in other places that I visited. Indeed, Scotland is ringing with songs and gladness to-day. Riding once from Ayr to Glasgow on a third-class train crowded with the "common people," who had been off on some excursion, my ears were filled all the way with the melody of those revival hymns, which rose ever and anon above the noise of the rushing train, and rang out clear and beautiful when we stopped for a few moments at the stations along the line. It seemed as though we were on board the very car of salvation, being speeded along by bands of singing angels come to convoy us.

Again, one Sunday evening I left my hotel in Glasgow to go to Dr. Andrew Bonar's church, some two miles distant. On my way I was treated to a novel spectacle, and one which was repeated every few hundred yards until I reached the church. I will describe it: I had gone but a little way from the hotel when my ears were greeted with the familiar strains:—

> "Safe in the arms of Jesus,
> Safe on His gentle breast,
> There by His love o'ershaded,
> Sweetly my soul shall rest."

Looking ahead of me I saw a crowd, from whence came the singing. Pressing up I joined the multitude of men, women and children gathered about a little band of brothers and sisters in the Lord, who were holding a service of song on the street corner. This little company could not *preach*, in the technical sense of that word, but they could *sing* the glad gospel out on the evening air, and thus say to all, "come!" I was very deeply impressed with their simple service, for they were evidently engaging in it as a matter that was to be done unto the Lord. As they passed from the singing of one hymn to another, sometimes slipping in a brief prayer between, I noted the effect upon the crowd. Though made up mostly of the street rabble, such as is seen only in the large cities of Great Britain, it was hushed into quiet, and even eager attention to the singing. My attention was called to some faces grown serious and thoughtful as they hearkened to words of love and hope, and more than once I saw the tears stealing down the grim cheek of some sinner unused to weep. Thus was God at work in those neglected hearts, and doubtless His dear love crept into many a soul through those songs. As I have already said, these singing bands with their attendant crowds were stationed all the way down the long street to the church, at intervals of a few hundred yards, and doubtless other of the principal streets of the city were similarly occupied. In no other way, it seems to me, could the gospel have been so effectually preached to that class of people.

At Dr. Bonar's church, which I reached at last, I found the same programme, only a little extended. There was no preacher—it was vacation time—but a few earnest brethren were occupying the platform, who in turn would speak a few words, perhaps relate some incident connected with the great revival, or rehearse the story of some remarkable conversion, and then a hymn would be announced—for instance:—

"I hear the Saviour say,
Thy strength indeed is small,"

and then the whole congregation worshiping God would fill the church with the sound of their song.

These incidents, as those of the other classes given above, might be multiplied, but perhaps enough has been said.

In concluding this letter, will it be out of place to express the hope and venture the prediction that this revival of sacred song is the forerunner or first fruits of a general revival of religion in the church of God? I believe it, and hail it as one who, watching for the morning, hails the gray dawn and roseate light in the East. "Even so, come Lord Jesus, come quickly."

INCIDENTS ASSOCIATED

WITH OUR

POPULAR HYMNS.

When Haydn was asked why his music was so cheerful, he replied, "I can't make any other. I write as I feel. When I think on God my heart is so full of joy that the notes dance and leap from my pen."

"We'll crowd thy gates with thankful songs,
High as the heavens our voices raise."

"Lord, teach our songs to rise;
Thy love can animate the strain,
And bid it *reach the skies.*"

"Learning here, by faith and love,
Songs of praise to sing above."

"The great salvation *loud proclaim,*
And shout for *joy* the Saviour's name."

"With calmly reverential joy,
Oh, let us all our lives employ
In setting forth thy love;
And raise in death our triumph higher,
And sing with all the heavenly choir,
The endless song above."

St. Augustine thus describes the effect which the music had upon him as he entered the church at Milan the first time after he was converted to Christianity: "The voices floated in at my ears, the truth was distilled at my heart, and the affection of piety overflowed in the sweet tears of joy."

HYMN INCIDENTS.

"I AM SO GLAD THAT OUR FATHER IN HEAVEN TELLS OF HIS LOVE IN THE BOOK HE HAS GIVEN."

THIS popular song, which was the rallying cry of the great revival in Scotland and also of many in America, was suggested to Mr. Bliss by hearing very frequently the chorus,—

"O how I love Jesus!"

He said to himself, "I have sung long enough of *my poor love for Christ*, and now I will sing of *His love for me*." He sat down and wrote the delightful and inspiring song of which the first verse is,—

"I am so glad that our Father in heaven
  Tells of his love in the Book he has given;
Wonderful things in the Bible I see,
  This is the dearest that *Jesus loves me*."

ONE Sunday a man came into our Sunday-school at the Boston North End Mission, drawn by the sweetness of the children's singing. He remained until the close, and came again that evening to our prayer-meeting. When the customary invitation to seek the Saviour was given, he came forward and found "peace in believing." To a few of us who had remained to pray with the penitent seekers he said, "My friends, I feel that I'm a saved man, and *I owe it to your children's singing 'Jesus loves me,' this afternoon.* I couldn't realize it, I've been such a miserable sinner; but after I went away I thought it over, 'Jesus loves me;' and then I thought of the next line, 'For the Bible tells me so,' and I tried to *believe* it, and I came here this evening to get you to pray for me." He became a regular attendant at the Mission, and while with us gave the clearest evidence of a genuine change of heart.

This is but one of very many similar instances of almost weekly occurrence at this Mission. This same man soon after felt called by the Holy Spirit to prepare himself for the Christian ministry, and at present he is regularly occupying a pulpit in Massachusetts, spending much of his time during the week in lecturing upon the evils of intemperance.

E. Tourjée.

At one of the revival meetings at Edinburgh a gay, giddy girl attended. She went late and was unable to get a seat, so she wandered about in the hall outside. Inside the church they were singing, led by Mr. Sankey: —

"Oh, I am so glad
That Jesus loves me,
Jesus loves me,
Jesus loves me."

The words went to her heart and her conscience, and she said, "I cannot sing that." When that meeting broke up she went to the meeting for anxious inquiries, and is now a rejoicing Christian.

A Missionary of the American Sunday-School Union in Missouri, after he had organized a Sunday-school recently, sang to them Mr. Bliss' delightful song,—

"I am so glad that Jesus loves me,"

and followed it with the question, "Are you glad? If not, why?" He had hardly finished when a young man rose, and rushing up to him, threw his arms around his neck, sobbing, "Oh, sir, you must not leave here till I'm a Christian!" Prayer was offered for him, and he was saved. Then he exclaimed, "Oh, that song! I could not get away from it and it has saved me."

A YOUNG woman in England went to a meeting where she heard Mr. Sankey singing this same hymn,—

"I am so glad that Jesus loves me,"

and while the hymn was being sung, began to feel for the first time in her life that she was a sinner. All her sins came up in array before her; and so numerous and aggravated did her sins appear, that she imagined she never could be saved. She said in her heart, "Jesus cannot love me. He could not love such a sinner as I." She went home in a state of extreme mental anguish, and did not sleep that night. Every opportunity of obtaining more light was eagerly seized. She took her place in the "Enquiry Room." There she found to her astonishment and joy that Jesus *could*, DID, DOES love sinners. She saw in God's opened Word that it was for sinners Jesus died, and for none others. When she realized this she too began to sing:

> "I am so glad that Jesus loves me,
> Jesus loves me, Jesus loves me, even me."

IN a praise meeting, during the recent revival services in Chicago, Mr. Sankey spoke as follows in regard to the power of this and other hymns:

"What I have to thank God especially for is the wonderful way He has used the power of song. I remember about five years ago coming to yonder depot one morning early. It was my first visit to this great city, and I knew none here save one man. I went along Madison Street, up State Street, to the North Side, and met my dear brother Moody. I had met him one year before in a distant State, while he was engaged in the work of the Master. As I went along those streets I recollect how I wondered if God had a work here for me in my coming to this city, or whether I had come on my own volition, and how while thinking in this way I sent up a prayer to God to bless me in the service in which I was about to engage. With thankfulness I remember the very first day I spent in this city. Somewhere down here we came among the sick and lowly, and went from one house to another singing and praying with the people; and what a blessing we received!

"God led us into other fields. I remember when the Tabernacle was rebuilt how I used to enjoy gathering the little people in, and teaching them those sweet songs that are already encircling the globe. Yes, encircling the globe, for but a few days ago I received a copy of these Gospel hymns printed in the Chinese language. They are sung in Africa and Asia, and are heard in France and Germany, England and America. I remember what peace and pleasure I had as I first taught these little hymns on the North Side. One day a lady called on me when I first had those classes, and said, 'There is a little singing girl belonging to one of your classes who is dying. She wants you to go and see her.' I went to her home — a little frame cottage, — and there I found a little maid dying — one whom I had known so well in the Thursday evening meetings. I said, 'My dear child, how is it with you?' 'Will you pray for my father and mother as you pray for us?" was the reply. 'But how is it with yourself?' I again asked. 'Oh, sir,' she answered, 'they tell me I am about to die, but I have found the Lord Jesus Christ.' 'When did you become a Christian?' I inquired. 'Don't you remember one Thursday when you were teaching me to sing —

"'"I am so glad that Jesus loves me,
Jesus loves me, Jesus loves me;"

and don't you remember how you told us that if we only gave our hearts to Him, He would love us? — and I gave it to Him.'

"What that little dying girl said to me helped to cheer me on more than anything I had heard before, because she was my first convert. Thank God, there have been many since."

"SOWING THE SEED BY THE DAYLIGHT FAIR."

In one of the temperance meetings connected with Mr. Moody's revival labors in Chicago, a very intelligent reformed drunkard attributed his reform to the influence of this hymn.

He confessed that it was difficult to speak about past experiences, especially when a man had been a heavy drinker, as he had been for sixteen years. He began sixteen years before by taking his first bottle of ale in the back room of a country store, and then, entering the army, he had plunged into dissipation, from which he thought at first he could free himself; but, as the years went by, he found the habit had become so strong that he couldn't control it, for it controlled him. He had stood at the mouth of the cannon, in front of the fixed bayonet, with the muzzle of a pistol right before him, and yet never had felt there such heart-sinking as he experienced when he began to realize what a man was, fettered by this vice. He came to this city some little time ago, and spent most of his days and nights in drinking and in playing cards, sometimes drinking thirty or forty drinks a day. While in this condition one night he came to the Tabernacle out of curiosity, to hear what was being said, and to see what was being done. He sat in the gallery, and was shielded by one of the long wooden pillars that upheld the roof. He saw the crowds enter with happy faces, and apparently light hearts, and nice clothes, and it hardened his heart, for he felt that he could never be like them. Then he heard Mr. Sankey sing the hymn "What Shall the Harvest Be?" It struck him when he heard the first verse:

> "Sowing the seed by the daylight fair,
> Sowing the seed by the noonday glare,
> Sowlng the seed by the fading light,
> Sowing the seed in the solemn night.
> Oh, what shall the harvest be?
> Oh, what shall the harvest be?"

And then, said he, Mr. Sankey sang the third verse, a verse that entered my heart. It roused me from my stupor. It brought me to feel what my own condition was, and these words entered my soul:

> "Sowing the seed of a lingering pain,
> Sowing the seed of a maddened brain,
> Sowing the seed of a tarnished name,
> Sowing the seed of eternal shame.
> Oh, what shall the harvest be?
> Oh, what shall *my* harvest be?"

During the recital of these lines, the speaker's voice trembled, his whole frame was agitated, his words and manner were impressed on his auditors, many of whom were moved to tears, and sobbing was audible in many parts of the great hall. He then went on to say that that night he had listened to this hymn, describing his own experience, he found no rest; the words seemed to meet him wherever he went,—

"What shall the harvest be?"

They were written on the walls of the room in the hotel where he boarded. They haunted him wherever he went. He tried to drown the voice by drinking heavier, but he couldn't remove them. There they were wherever he turned,—

"What shall the harvest be?"

He left the Tabernacle saying to himself he would never return; but finally, such was his unrest, he went into the inquiry-room, and talked with Mr. Farwell and Mr. Brewster, and after a great struggle he gave himself to Christ. He trusted in the salvation wrought out for him, and, though he had lost position, home, family by the accursed cup, he rejoiced that God had looked down on him and saved him.

"WHAT MEANS THIS EAGER, ANXIOUS THRONG?"

—*Rev. E. P. Hammond.*

PERHAPS no hymn has been oftener sung during the last ten years in evangelistic meetings than the one with the above heading. It will be interesting to many to learn the circumstances which suggested it. It was originally written as a description of the powerful revival of religion in Newark, N. J., in 1864, when hundreds were led by the Holy Spirit to find peace and joy in believing in Jesus.

It was on a Saturday afternoon, when one of the largest churches was crowded with children and adults, that R. G. Pardee, that dear man who has done so much for Sunday-schools in America, made some very impressive remarks on the answer given to blind Bartimeus in Luke xviii. 37: "They told him that Jesus of Nazareth passeth by."

Miss Campbell was present, and shortly after wrote those words which have been sung by thousands and tens of thousands the world over. It struck me that they might be set to music, and I found they went very well to the tune, "Sweet Hour of Prayer." There were originally nine verses, if I remember rightly, but I only printed seven in the *New Praises of Jesus*. It has always been popular in evangelistic meetings, and multitudes by it have been awakened, and led to cry out, as did the blind man, "Jesus, thou son of David, have mercy on me."

I remember that a gambler came into a morning meeting, which crowded a Congregational church in Lockport, N. Y., while we were singing that hymn, and at the close of it, though it was the first meeting he had attended, he arose, and with tears streaming down his cheeks, begged the Christians to pray for him. Earnest prayer at once ascended in his behalf, and it was answered. A few nights after, in relating his experience before a great audience in Dr. Wisner's church, he referred to this hymn as having been the means of awakening him, and added:

"As I went out of the church that day, and over the canal, I threw the 'Devil's Testament,' with its fifty-two leaves into it."

I am sure he never played a card afterwards He lived a consistent Christian life, and has since died a happy death. I might fill pages relating similar instances to illustrate the good this hymn has accomplished. Night after night during the past winter, not only in Great Britain, under the leadership of Brother Sankey, but also in California and Oregon, it has been sung by thousands who will remember it to all eternity. The verses together are a sermon in themselves.

Prof. Theo. E. Perkins has written some very appropriate music for this hymn, which is a favorite with Mr. Sankey, and is often heard at Brother Moody's revival meetings.

It is my earnest prayer that multitudes more may be led by this hymn so earnestly to call upon the Saviour, that they, too, may receive their sight, and hear Him saying: "Thy faith hath saved thee."

"I HEAR THE SAVIOUR SAY," AND "THERE IS A GATE THAT STANDS AJAR."

Maggie Lindsay, a girl of seventeen, who had been for some time a pupil-teacher in the Free Church Normal Seminary, Edinburgh, found the Saviour in the Free Assembly Hall, on the last night of 1873. On the 27th of January following she was journeying by train to Aberdeen, when a terrible accident took place at Manuel, near Linlithgow. She was amongst those who were most seriously injured, both legs being broken, and a rib, with other wounds of a painful character. Her sufferings were acute, but she bore up under them with "gentle Christian heroism," as an eye-witness testifies; such as drew forth the admiration of all around. When the terrible crash on the railroad happened, she had been reading Mr. Sankey's hymn-book, and there was the mark of a turned-down leaf at her favorite hymn, "The Gates Ajar," with its touching refrain,—

"Oh, depths of mercy! can it be
That gate was left ajar for me?"

During her last hours it was affecting to hear her, amidst so great suffering, sing softly to herself,—

"For me, for me?"

Another hymn-book, "Phillips' Hallowed Songs," was recovered from the *débris*, "its pages stained with her own blood." "At one time," writes the minister who attended her during the last moments of life, "when we thought she had fallen into a sleep, eagerly wished and prayed for by us, we moved away out of sight. But in a few minutes we heard her, in low, gentle tones, singing to herself the words,—

'Nothing, either great or small,
Remains for me to do;
Jesus died, and paid it all,
All the debt I owe.'

Shortly afterwards she fell asleep in Jesus. 'Blessed are the dead that die in the Lord.'"

"YET THERE IS ROOM! THE LAMB'S BRIGHT HALL OF SONG."

A GAY, thoughtless young woman, in Scotland, was one day invited by an acquaintance to accompany her to a Moody and Sankey meeting. She declined to go, saying she did not care to hear Moody and Sankey. On being further pressed, she consented and went. She was not impressed by anything she heard in the course of the meeting. Indeed, she thought there was "nothing in it," and wondered why people should make so much ado about what seemed so commonplace. The last hymn, "Yet there is Room" was being sung by Mr. Sankey alone. He had reached the last stanza —

"Ere night that gate may close, and seal thy doom,
Then the last, low, long cry, 'No room, no room!'
No room, no room; oh, woful cry, 'No room!'"

These last words of Dr. Bonar's hymn fell upon the ear of the young woman like a sudden thunder-clap. She left the meeting, but the words went with her. "No room, no room!" still rang in her ears. Conscience awoke at the sound of this warning bell. Nor could she rest, until, as she trusts, she found rest in the great Redeemer.

"COME HOME! COME HOME!"

IN Victoria Hall, Sunderland, England, Mr. Moody one evening closed his sermon with the story of a prodigal son, who was reconciled to his father — as he stood by the bed of his dying mother. Then Mr. Sankey sang,—

"Oh, prodigal child, come home."

When the audience had been dismissed, there came into the enquiry meeting a young man who had long played the part of the prodigal son, to the great grief of his godly parents. With a face marked with deepest penitence he came up to his father and mother, and throwing his arms about them, with many tears asked their forgiveness and also the pardon of God for his sins. The prodigal child had a double welcome from God and man.

> "Come home! come home!
> You are weary at heart,
> For the way has been dark,
> And so lonely and wild,
> O prodigal child!
> Come home, oh come home!

"HOLD THE FORT."

WHEN General Sherman was marching "from Atlanta to the Sea," he left a detachment of troops at a certain fort in his rear. By some means the enemy got behind him, attacked the fort and drove its defenders from the outer to the inner intrenchments. The commanding officer was about to run up the white flag, when he saw on a distant hill the signal, "*Hold the fort: I am coming, Sherman.*" This incident gave to Mr. Bliss the idea of his well known hymn, "Hold the fort."

WHILE Mr. Moody was in Dublin, the Royal Circus was much less attended than usual, and so, a month or two afterward, the clowns made a plan to ridicule the evangelists. At one of their entertainments, in the presence of a large concourse, one clown said to the other, "I'm rather *Moody* to-night; how do you feel?" The other replied, "I feel rather *Sankey-monius*, myself." The fun did not work, at least, not as the clowns expected. The audience hissed them out of the ring and struck up,—

"Hold the fort, for I am coming,"

in which all the people joined, and thus ended the effort to make sport of the evangelists.

"Ho! my comrades, see the signal
Waving in the sky!
Reinforcements now appearing,
Victory is nigh!"

Chorus.

"'Hold the fort, for I am coming,"
Jesus signals still,
Wave the answer back to Heaven,
'By thy grace we will.'"

"BRIGHTLY BEAMS OUR FATHER'S MERCY."

On a dark stormy night, when the waves rolled like mountains, and not a star was to be seen, a boat, rocking and plunging, near the Cleveland harbor.

"Are you sure this is Cleveland?" asked the Captain, seeing only one light from the lighthouse.

"Quite sure, sir," replied the pilot.

"Where are the lower lights?"

"Gone out, sir."

"Can you make the harbor?"

"We *must*, or perish, sir!"

And with a strong hand and a brave heart the old pilot turned the wheel. But, alas, in the darkness he missed the channel, and with a crash upon the rocks the boat was shivered, and many a life lost in a watery grave. Brethren, the Master will take care of the great light-house; *let us keep the lower lights burning!*

"Mr. Bliss, hearing this story from Mr. Moody wrought out its moral in his well-known song,—

"Let the lower lights be burning!
Send a gleam across the wave!
Some poor fanting, struggling seaman,
You may rescue, you may save."

"LIGHT IN THE DARKNESS, SAILOR."

THIS song is founded on the following incident:

"We watched the wreck with great anxiety. The life-boat had been out some hours, but could not reach the vessel through the great breakers that raged and foamed on the sand-bank. The boat appeared to be leaving the crew to perish. But in a few minutes the captain and sixteen sailors were taken off, and the vessel went down.

"When the life-boat came to you, did you expect it had brought some tools to repair your old ship?' I said.

"'Oh, no; she was a total wreck. Two of her masts were gone, and if we had stayed mending her only a few minutes, we must have gone down, sir.'

"'When once off the old wreck and safe in the life-boat what remained for you to do?'

"'Nothing, sir, but just to pull for the shore.'"

"Light in the darkness, sailor, day is at hand!
See o'er the foaming billows fair Haven's land,
Drear was the voyage, sailor, now almost o'er,
Safe within the life-boat, sailor, pull for the shore."

"ONLY AN ARMOR-BEARER."

THIS song was suggested by the familiar incident of Jonathan and his armor-bearer:

"Now it came to pass upon a day, that Jonathan, the son of Saul, said unto the young man that bare his armor, Come and let us go over to the Philistines' garrison, that is on the other side: it may be that the Lord will work for us: for there is no restraint to the Lord to save by many or by few. And his armor-bearer said unto him, "Do all that is in thine heart; turn thee: behold I am with thee according to thy heart. And Jonathan climbed up upon his hands and upon his feet, and his armor-bearer after him: and they fell before Jonathan; and his armor-bearer slew after him.

"So the Lord saved Israel that day: and the battle passed over to Beth-aven."

"Only an armor-bearer, proudly I stand,
Waiting to follow at the King's command;
Marching if 'onward' shall the order be,
Standing by my Captain, serving faithfully."

"I AM COMING TO THE CROSS."

AT Glasgow, one evening at eight o'clock, there was a vast assembly, of *men only*, in the

City Hall. They were packed into every corner; and outside were nearly as many in vain seeking entrance. It was a memorable time. Mr. Moody's subject was, "Whosoever,"—salvation absolutely free, all gift; nothing between a sinner and eternal life but an unbroken will. The mass of men listened with intense interest; now and then you could see a tear, or the head bent in deep emotion. When Mr. Sankey sang the hymn, "I am Coming to the Cross," nothing could exceed the rapt, silent attention. When he came to the verse,—

"In the promises I trust,
  Now I feel the blood applied:
I am prostrate in the dust,
  I with Christ am crucified,"

not a head in the vast multitude moved, every face expressed deep feeling. This verse was repeated amid still deeper silence and emotion. At the close, when an invitation was given to those who minded to remain for twenty minutes simply for prayer, above a thousand remained, and thereafter a large number waited for conversation, although the hour was late.

"RING THE BELLS OF HEAVEN."

An English writer gives a touching incident connected with this hymn from the dying hours of a Christian child of ten years.

She much delighted in Mr. Sankey's hymns. "Oh, how I love those dear hymns!" — mentioning, "Safe in the arms of Jesus," and others.

"When I am gone, mother, will you ask the girls of the school to sing that hymn? —

"'Ring the bells of Heaven! there is joy to-day
For a soul returning from the wild!
See! the Father meets him out upon the way,
Welcoming his weary, wandering child!

Chorus.

"'Glory! glory! how the angels sing!
Glory! glory! how the loud harps ring!'
'Tis the ransomed army, like a mighty sea,
Pealing forth the anthem of the free.

"Ring the bells of heaven! spread the feast to-day,
Angels, swell the glad triumphant strain!
Tell the joyful tidings, bear it far away!
For a precious soul is born again."

The night before her death she said,—

"Dear father and mother, I hope I shall meet you in Heaven. I am *so* happy, mother! You cannot think how light and happy I feel!"

Again: "Perhaps Jesus may send me to fetch some of my brothers and sisters; I hope He will send me to fetch *you*, mother."

Half an hour before her departure she exclaimed, "*Oh, mother, hark at the bells of heaven! they are ringing so beautifully!*"

Then, closing her eyes awhile, presently she cried again, "Hearken to the harps! they are most splendid! Oh, I wish you could hear them!"

Then, shortly after, she spoke again:

"Oh, mother, I see the Lord Jesus, and the angels! Oh, if you could see them too! He is sending one to fetch me!"

She had been counting the hours and minutes since she heard the mill-bell at 1.30 p.m., longing so earnestly to depart; yet expressed a hope she might see her dear father (then absent at work) before she went.

At last, just five minutes or so before her expiring breath, she said,—

"Oh, mother, lift me up from the pillow—*high*, high up! Oh, I wish you could lift me *right up* into heaven!" Then, almost immediately after—as, doubtless, conscious that the parting moment was at hand, — "Put me down again — down, quick!"

And then, calmly, brightly, joyously gazing upward, as at some vision of surprising beauty, she peacefully, sweetly, triumphantly breathed forth her precious spirit into the arms of the ministering angel whom her Jesus had sent to fetch her, and so was forever with the Lord she loved.

"IN THE CHRISTIAN'S HOME IN GLORY."

IN one of Mr. Moody's meetings, in England, a speaker rose and said that he had been an actor on the English stage for some years and had written plays. He was one night entertaining a London theatre audience, when suddenly a hymn he had learned in childhood came to his mind, beginning,—

> "In the Christian's home in glory,
> There remains a land of rest,"

which so unmanned him that he was compelled to go to the manager and tell him that he could not go on. He stifled conviction however, by drinking heavily at the bar of the theatre. The religious impression then overcome he said had been renewed by the words of Mr. Moody and Mr. Sankey and he had now given himself to Christ.

A CHRISTIAN boy of Rev. Dr. Talmage's Sunday-school, when about to die, said to his mother, "Don't cry, but sing; sing,—

'There is rest for the weary;'"

and when they had sung a verse, he put his wasted hand over his heart, and said, just before it ceased its beating,—

"There is rest for me."

THE CHRISTIAN'S HOME.

In the Christian's home in glory
There remains a land of rest;
There my Saviour's gone before me,
To fulfil my soul's request.

Chorus.

There is rest for the weary,
There is rest for the weary,
There is rest for you;
On the other side of Jordan,
In the sweet fields of Eden,

Where the tree of life is blooming,
  There is rest for you.

He is fitting up a mansion,
  Which eternally shall stand;
For my stay shall not be transient
  In that holy, happy land.

Sing, O sing, ye heirs of glory!
  Shout your triumphs as you go;
Zion's gates will open for you,
  You shall find an entrance through.

"LORD, I HEAR OF SHOWERS OF BLESSING."

THE singing leader in an inland Sunday-school was a man of skeptical tendencies, — moral and upright, though far from being a Christian. One Sunday this hymn was commenced as usual, but when the leader came to the passage,—

"Pass me not, O tender Saviour,
  Let me love and cling to Thee;
I am longing for Thy favor;
  Whilst Thou'rt calling, oh, call me."

his voice quivered, his frame shook, and in anguish he cried out, "Pray for me." It was a scene of thrilling interest, and earnest prayers then went up from teachers and scholars that he who had so long sung the sweet songs of Zion without feeling their power, might now sing with the spirit and the understanding. He was happily converted, and is now a faithful Christian.

"SAFE IN THE ARMS OF JESUS."

—*Fannie J. Crosby.*

NOT long ago we visited from time to time, till the end came, a bright young life that had been laid hold of by our great British disease, consumption. Insidious, but terribly sure, were the advances made by this fell waster; and the watching was all the more solemn because the indications of spiritual life were but faint and dubious. Not many weeks before the close, a young lady, one of the recent converts, found her way to this stricken one, and began a series of visits which were most welcome. In the visitor the dying young woman found one younger than herself, who could sing *from experience*, "Safe in the arms of Jesus;" one to whose sweet voice she listened with pleasure, so far as the disease permitted; one whom she soon loved. It is not permitted us to see into the hearts of others ; but this seemed evident in the case of the poor sufferer now alluded to, that more than any other influence brought to bear upon her, the hymns, words, and visits of the young lady created a longing to know Jesus as her own Saviour.

During the revival meetings in Edinburgh, a young man, who was an avowed skeptic, came into one of the meetings to scoff at all he might hear. He said afterwards,—

"I believed only in God and the devil; the latter I served well and sat laughing at the Christians about me whom I thought nothing better than fools."

At length that beautiful hymn,—

"Safe in the arms of Jesus,"

was sung. A sudden thrill passed through his whole frame and then, like a dart went to his his very soul. His feelings were awful, but he listened to the next verse and he felt, "There is a Saviour. Who is He? Where is He?" He quickly realized the truth that *Jesus was his Saviour* and he threw himself into His arms, and left the place, saying in his new joy and zeal, "I will now live and work for Jesus."

"TO-DAY THE SAVIOUR CALLS."

ON the night when the great Chicago fire broke out Mr. Moody spoke to an audience of three thousand people, urging, as usual, immediate decision for Christ.

The song was then sung,—

> "To-day the Saviour calls:
> Ye wand'rers come."

Ten persons stayed to give themselves to Christ, in response to this hymn. At the close of the enquiry meeting as they went out into the street they say the whole sky lighten up with the blaze of burning buildings. Three, at least, of those ten persons perished in the fire. One more refusal to accept Christ and it would have been too late.

"I GAVE MY LIFE FOR THEE."

THE beautiful song of which this is the first line, was suggested by the motto, "This I did for thee," which a German clergyman placed under a print of "Christ on the Cross," that hung in his study. It is said that Count Zinzendorf, of precious memory, was first taught to love the Saviour by reading this motto.

DURING a Western Sunday-school Convention, there arose a cry of dissatisfaction, "A ring!" "A ring!" The strange and false charge was made that the managers were conducting the convention according to some recent scheme. Quite a discordant excitement ensued, during which a distinguished singer who was present, was called on to sing. He sang,—

"All this I did for thee,
My precious blood I shed
That thou might'st ransomed be,
And rescued from the dead;
All this I did for thee —
What hast thou done for me?"

Through the song Christ seemed to whisper to the discordant convention, "Peace, be still," and when the song had ceased, a calm, Christ-like spirit had filled the convention and continued with it to the end.

"JESUS, LOVER OF MY SOUL."

—*Charles Wesley.*

ABOUT the time that Isaac Watts was writing his earliest hymns at Southampton, in Southern England, two brothers were born in the little town of Epworth, who were destined to be better known over the world than any other two men whom Britain produced in that half century. While their godly mother (Susannah) was dying, she said to her weeping household, "My children, as soon as my spirit is released, sing a song of praise to God." Among the group who joined in this song of triumph with faltering voices, were John, the founder of Methodism, and Charles, its sweet singer. John was system; Charles was song. John was the Bezaleel who laid the foundations, and hewed out the pillars of the new tabernacle; but Charles was the Asaph who filled it with melody.

Methodism was builded rapidly; but the walls never would have gone up so fast had they not been built to music. Charles Wesley was a born poet. Like Toplady, he was all nerve and fire and enthusiasm. God gave him a musical ear, intense emotions, ardent affections, and a glowing piety that never grew cold. He ate, drank, slept and dreamed nothing but hymns!

He must have been the ready writer of at least four thousand hymns. One day, while on his itineracy, his pony stumbled, and threw him off. The only record he makes of the accident in his diary is this: "My companions thought I had broken my neck; but my leg only was bruised, my hand sprained, and my head stunned, which spoiled my making hymns until—*next day!*" Truly a man must have been possessed with a master passion, who could have written a sentence like that.

Wesley found his inspirations "on every hedge."

He threw off hymns as Spurgeon throws off sermons. For example, when he was preaching to a crowd of rude stonecutters and quarrymen at Portland, he turned his appeal into metre, and improvised a hymn, in which occur the vigorous lines:—

"Come, O thou all-victorious Lord,
Thy power to us make known;
Strike with the hammer of thy word,
And break these hearts of stone."

Standing once on the dizzy promontory of Land's End, and looking down into the boiling waves on each side of the cliff, he broke out into these solemn and thrilling words: —

"Lo! on a narrow rock of land,
'Twixt two unbounded seas I stand,
Yet how insensible."

For every scene and circumstance of life, for prayer-meetings, for watch nights, for love feasts, and for dying hours and funerals, he had a holy impassioned lay. But, like Watts, Cowper and Toplady, he had his master-piece. The Lord of glory bestowed on Charles Wesley the high honor of composing the finest heart-hymn in the English tongue. If the greatest hymn of the cross is "Rock of Ages," and the greatest hymn of providence is Cowper's "God moves in a mysterious way," and the grandest battle-hymn is Martin Luther's "God is our refuge," then it may be said, also, that the queen of all the lays of holy love is that immortal song: —

> "Jesus, lover of my soul!
> Let me to Thy bosom fly,
> While the billows near me roll,
> While the tempest still is high!"

Whatever may be said of Wesley's doctrine of perfect holiness, there is not much doubt that he attained "unto perfection" when he wrote this hymn. It is happily married, also, to two exquisite tunes, "Refuge and Martyn," both of which are worthy of the alliance. The first of these tunes is a gem. The one central, all pervading idea of this matchless hymn is the soul's yearning for its Saviour.

The figures of speech vary, but not the thought. In one line we see a storm-tossed voyager crying out for shelter, until the tempest is over. In another line we see a timid, tearful child, nestling in its mother's arms, with the words faltering on its tongue,—

> "Let me to Thy bosom fly!
> Hangs my helpless soul on Thee!"

Two lines of the hymn have been breathed fervently and often out of bleeding hearts. When we were once in the valley of the death-shade, with one beautiful child in its new-made grave, and the other threatened with fatal disease, there was no prayer which we uttered oftener than this,—

"Leave, ah! leave me not alone;
Still support and comfort me."

We do not doubt that tens of thousands of other bereaved and wounded hearts have cried this piercing cry, out of the depths,—

"Still support and comfort me."

The whole hymn is at once a confession and a prayer. It is a prayer in metre. And no man is prepared to sing these words aright unless his soul is filled with deepest and most earnest longing after the Lord Jesus. What an awful blasphemy it is for unsanctified singers in a choir to perform this holy prayer merely as a feat of musical skill.

What college boy would dare to commit to memory the Lord's prayer, and speak it as a mere piece of declamation on the stage? Yet we do not see any difference between declaiming a prayer, and the heartless mockery of performing, for musical effect, such words,—

"Hide me, O my Saviour, hide,
Till the storm of life is past!"

Or that self-surrender for the dying hour,—

"Oh, receive my soul at last!"

Words like these are too infinitely solemn for frivolous lips in the concert-room or the organ-loft. When a congregation sings such a hymn as "Jesus, lover of my soul," each person should feel as if he were uttering a fervent personal prayer to the Son of God.

The history of Charles Wesley's incomparable hymn would fill a volume. Millions have sung it, and will be singing it when the millennial morn breaks.

A coasting vessel once went on the rocks in a gale, in the British Channel. The captain and crew took to the boats and were lost. They might have been saved had they remained on board; for a huge wave carried the vessel up among the rocks, where the ebbing tide left her high and dry. In the captain's cabin a hymn-book was found lying on his table. It was opened to a particular page, and the pencil still lay in it which had marked the favorite lines of the stout sailor, who was just about going into the jaws of death. While the hurricane was howling outside, the captain had drawn his pencil beside these glorious words of cheer,—

> "Jesus, lover of my soul,
> Let me to thy bosom fly,
> While the billows near me roll,
> While the tempest still is high!
> Hide me, O my Saviour hide,
> Till the storm of life is past;
> Safe into the haven guide,
> Oh, receive my soul at last!"

Blessed death song! Thousands of God's redeemed ones have shouted it forth as the "haven" of rest opened its celestial glories to their view. If we could choose the manner of our departure, we would wish to die singing,—

> "Other refuge have I none;
> Hangs my helpless soul on Thee!
> Leave, ah, leave me not alone,
> Still support and comfort me;
> All my trust on Thee is stayed,
> All my help from Thee I bring;
> Cover my defenseless head,
> With the shadow of Thy wing."

—*Rev. T. L. Cuyler, D. D., in "Heart Life."*

Mr. Long of Philadelphia in his work on hymnology gives the following incident as the occasion of the hymn :

The brothers John and Charles Wesley, with Richard Pilmore, were one evening holding a twilight meeting on the common, when they were attacked by a mob and fled from its fury for their lives. The first place of refuge that they found, after having been for some time separated, was a hedge-row near at hand, behind which they hid a few minutes, protecting themselves from serious injury by the missiles that fell like hail about them, by clasping their hands above their heads as they lay with their faces in the dust. As night drew on, the darkness enabled them to leave their temporary retreat for a safer one at some distance. They found their way at last to a spring-house, where, in comparative security, they waited for their pursuers to weary of seeking them. "Here they struck a light with a flint-stone," dusted their sóiled and tattered garments, and, after quenching their thirst, bathed their hands and faces in the water that bubbled from the spring and flowed away in a sparkling streamlet. Then it was that

Charles Wesley was inspired to white, "Jesus, lover of my soul," with a bit of lead he had hammered into a pencil.

These circumstances beautifully illustrate the hymn, giving to almost every line a reality that makes it peculiarly significant to every loving Christian heart. They had fled before their enemies, and found shelter from danger: he sang:

> "Jesus, lover of my soul,
> *Let me* to thy bosom *fly*."

No figure is so commonly used with reference to the assaults of the wicked as that of the line:

> "While the nearer waters roll,"

which is a favorite with the psalmist. The next line

> "While the *tempest* still is high;"

also reminds one of the sweet songs of Israel, but seems above the former appropriate, recalling, as it does, the storm of missiles that broke upon the hedge when they were concealed behind it. The same figure, carried still further finds expression in the rest of the first stanza:

> "Hide me, O my Saviour hide,
> Till the storm of life is past!

> *Safe into the haven* guide,
> O receive my soul at last!"

There can be no doubt but that the little spring-house suggested "the haven of eternal rest" for which the soul of the persecuted evangelist longed with unutterable desire. They had barely escaped death by flying to the only place of safety within their reach; what wonder then that the poet should exclaim,—

> "*Other refuge have I none,*
> Hangs my helpless soul on thee:"

as he thought, with a shudder, of the loneliness of the first of their flight, which is touchingly indicated in the lines,—

> "Leave, oh, *leave me not alone,*
> Still support and comfort me!"

The thought of the first two lines of this second stanza is repeated in the fifth and sixth, and followed by yet another reference to the period of their greatest peril. Christ, the *only* hope of a sinner, is addressed in the words,—

> "*All my trust* in thee is stayed,
> *All my help* from thee I bring!"

and entreated to save his soul when imperilled, as their bodies had been. He prays,—

"*Cover my* defenceless *head,*
With the shadow of thy wing!"

The third verse which is usually omitted, is a passionate appeal for aid in weakness and exhaustion:

"Wilt thou not regard my call?
Wilt thou not accept my prayer?
Lo! *I sink, I faint, I fall!*
Lo! on thee I cast my care!"

together, perhaps, with a reminiscence of the aid which they were doubtless able to render one another:

"*Reach me out thy* gracious *hand!*
While I of thy strength receive,
Hoping against hope I stand.
Dying, and behold I live?"

The sufficiency of the Saviour in implied comparison with any human helper, is finely brought out by the poet who, like Paul, evidently glories in his own weakness:

"*Thou,* O Christ, *art all I want;*
More than all in thee I find;
Raise the *fallen,* cheer the *faint,*
Heal the sick and lead the blind;
Just and holy is thy name;
I am all unrighteousness;

> False and full of sin I am,
> Thou art full of truth and grace!"

The weakness of their condition recalls its cause, the "wounds and bruises" that have ever been symbolical of sin. These had been laved in the limpid water flowing at their feet, hence the strain,—

> "Plenteous grace in thee is found,
> Grace to cover all my sin;
> *Let the* healing *stream abound,*
> *Make* and keep me *pure* within!"

They had drank, too, of the water, and as it had refreshed their fainting bodies, would the Christian take refreshment from the water of life. This thought furnished the climax of the hymn, than which a more inspiring could hardly be framed in words. It is the language of perfect confidence in the Redeemer as the source of eternal life. He sings, O how sublimely!

> "Thou of life the *fountain* art;
> Freely let me take of thee;
> *Spring* thou *up* within my heart,
> Rise to all eternity!"

A VERY touching incident in the last days of

the life of the late President Finney has just appeared. It was the Sabbath. After tea, according to his custom, he was walking about his grounds with his wife enjoying a glowing sky and a cool refreshing breeze. Evening worship in the church near at hand, which he himself had planned and in which he had preached nearly forty years, had just begun. Presently there came floating out of the old sanctuary the familiar strains of the dear old hymn,—

"Jesus, lover of my soul,
Let me to thy bosom fly,
Where the nearer waters roll,
While the tempest still is high:
Hide me, O my Saviour hide,
Till the storm of life is past;
Safe into the haven guide,
O receive my soul at last.

"Other refuge have I none,
Hangs my helpless soul on thee:
Leave, oh, leave me not alone,
Still support and comfort me.
All my trust on thee is stayed
All my help from thee I bring;
Cover my defenceless head
With the shadow of thy wing."

He quickly caught it, devoutly joined the invisible congregation and kept them company to the end. Before the morning dawned the prayer then breathed was answered, and he who had so long trusted in Christ was "at last." received into the bosom of his Saviour.

A FINE, intelligent Virginian young man, while residing in the West, became an infidel and a blasphemer of the name of God. From this state he was delivered by reading the work of Soame Jenyns; but, while he acquiesced in the truth of revelation, he yet did not feel its power. He was attacked by a lingering and fatal disease, which led him to reflection and prayer, but often made it difficult for him to converse. Three Christian friends sometimes visited him, to beguile the tedious hours by singing. They one day entered his room, and, almost without any previous remarks, began the hymn,—

"There is a fountain filled with blood,"

and then,—

"The voice of free grace cries, Escape to the mountain."

He then said to them, "There is nothing I so much delight to hear as the first hymn you ever sung to me,—

'Jesus, lover of my soul.'"

We began to sing it to the tune of *Martyn*, and found the solemnity which had reigned in the little circle while singing the two former hymns began to be changed to weeping. We struck the touching strains of the second stanza, and the weeping became loud; the heart of him who had reviled Christ broke; and we feared that to sing the remaining stanza would be more than he could bear. When singing in his room a few days after this, he said, "I don't think I shall ever hear 'Jesus, lover of my soul' sung again: it so excites me that my poor body cannot bear it."

SEVERAL years ago, a ship was burned near the English Channel. Among the passengers were a father, mother, and their little child, a daughter not many months old. When the discovery was made that the ship was on fire, and the alarm was given, there was great confusion, and this family became separated. The father was rescued, and taken to Liverpool; but the mother and infant were carried overboard by the crowd, and, unnoticed by those who were doing all in their power to save the sufferers still on the ship, they drifted out of the channel with the tide, the mother clinging to a fragment of the wreck, with her little one clasped to her breast.

Late in the afternoon of that day, a vessel bound from Newport, Wales, to America, was moving slowly along in her course. There was only a slight breeze, and the captain was impatiently walking the deck, when his attention was called to an object some distance off, which looked like a person in the water. The officers and crew watched it for a time, and as no vessel was near from which any one could have fallen overboard, they thought it impossible that this could be a human being. But, as their vessel was scarcely moving, it was thought best to get out a boat and row to the object. The boat was accordingly lowered and manned. It was watched with considerable interest by those who remained on board, and they noticed that, as it drew near to the drifting speck, the rowers rested on their oars two or three minutes, then moved forward, took in the object or thing, they knew not which, and returned to the ship. When the boat's crew came on board, they brought with them this mother and her child, alive and well; and the sailors said that, as they drew near, they heard a female voice sweetly singing. As with a common impulse, the men ceased rowing and listened, and then the words of the beautiful hymn, sung by this trusting Christian, all unconscious that deliverance was so near, came over the waves to their ears: —

"Jesus, lover of my soul,
  Let me to Thy bosom fly,
While the waters near me roll,
  While the tempest still is high!
Hide me, O my Saviour, hide,
  Till the storm of life is past;
Safe into the haven guide,
  Oh, receive my soul at last.

Other refuge have I none,
  Hangs my helpless soul on thee!
Leave, ah, leave me not alone,

Still support and comfort me;
All my trust on Thee is stayed,
All my help from Thee I bring;
Cover my defenseless head,
With the shadow of Thy wing."

In due time the vessel arrived in America. The mother wrote to her friends in England, and thus the father learned of the safety of his wife and child, and in about four months from the time of their separation they were happily reunited.

A POOR woman, who had no hope in Christ, was dying in the attic of one of the New York tenement houses. A minister was sent for, but his words and prayers failed to give her hope. She said again and again, as he talked to her, "It's no use; I'm too wicked, and it's too late." At length he began to sing, "Jesus, lover of my soul," and sang two verses. Noticing her deep interest, he turned to her and said, "Can't you trust him now?" With a smile of joy she replied, "*Other refuge have I none.*" Her happy face showed her acceptance of Jesus.

We were a happy company of Sunday-school scholars and friends on Lake Winnipeseogee. The day had been spent most pleasantly. The "Lady of the Lake" had come alongside the wharf and with a clear, sharp note from her clarion bell had invited us again on board. Friends from shore and on the water waved their friendly "good-by." Seated upon the upper deck, anticipating a most charming ride upon the lake, the fastenings were unloosed and we shot out upon the clear ample waters, and were fairly on our course, anticipating an hour's enjoyment only afforded by such a company and such an occasion. All at once we were confronted by one of the most terrific storms of wind, rain, lightning and thunder ever known by the captain of the boat in an experience of twenty-five years.

Terror now took possession of nearly all, as well it might. In a confusion amounting almost to a panic, all rushed for the cabin's hold. Happening to be among the last to leave the deck, and standing about midway on the stairs, we witnessed a scene such as we had never beheld before, and never wish to re-experience. Women were crying and fainting, children were frantic with fright, and strong, full-grown men stood pale and trembling. We tried to inspire calmness and composure, but to very little purpose. We remembered being in the coliseum at Boston on the 4th of July of last year, when a terrible hurricane and storm burst upon us. What seemed an inevitable and fearful panic, was turned into huzzas when the English band changed from a classic selection to our own patriotic "Yankee Doodle." We did not strike up any of the national airs, but just what was in our heart at the time,—

> "I am trusting, Lord, in thee,
> Dear Lamb of Calvary."

The sentiment found a response in other hearts; we did not sing alone. Others joined, and our voices were above the tumult within and the roar of the hurricane without, and there was a calm. But without, the storm raged with increased fury, and its roar was fearful. Then we sang,—

> "Jesus, lover of my soul,
> Let me to try bosom fly."

The lightning's flash seemed almost to envelope

us in a sheet of flame, and the thunders seemed to shake the earth and sea. And then we sang,—

"Other refuge have I none;
Hangs my helpless soul on thee."

The gallant boat, in whose palpitating bosom we had taken refuge, met the storm bravely, but the gale was too mighty; she was beaten back by the buffeting winds and waves, and imperilled by hidden rocks; and then we sang,—

"Thou, O Christ, art all I want,
More than all in Thee I find."

But the heart of the hurricane began to be touched and the winds to relent; the lightning had a softer glare, and the thunder fell more tenderly in our ears; so we sang,—

"Ere we reach the shining river,
Lay we every burden down,
Grace our spirits shall deliver,
And provide a robe and crown."

Now there is a calm. The hurricane has sped on with its accompaniment of flood and terror, and has left us out in the full clear sunshine. The shore and destination is in view towards sunset; and now we will sing,—

> "Land ahead, its fruits are waving,"

and we ring out the chorus,—

> "Rocks and storms I'll fear no more,
> When on that eternal shore."

And now the "Lady of the Lake," in her grandest majesty, sweeps in graceful curve to make her landing, when again we all sang,—

> "Now we're safe from all temptation,
> All the storms of life are past,"

and the

> "Rocks and storms we'll fear no more;
> When on that eternal shore,
> Drop the anchor, furl the sail;
> I am safe within the veil."

The singing saved us from a panic; and, saved from that, we were saved from consequences we dared not contemplate. The twilight found us all safe at our homes.

Other refuge have I none,
  Hangs my helpless soul on Thee;
Leave, ah, leave me not alone,
  Sfill support and comfort me;
All my trust on Thee is stayed,
  All my help from Thee I bring;
Cover my defenseless head,
  With the shadow of Thy wing.

A CHAPLAIN in our army one morning found Tom, the drummer-boy, a great favorite with all the men, and whom, because of his sobriety and religious example, they called "the young deacon," sitting alone under a tree. At first he thought him asleep, but, as he drew near, the boy lifted up his head, and he saw tears in his eyes.

"Well, Tom, my boy, what is it; for I see your thoughts are sad? What is it?"

"Why, sir, I had a dream last night, which I can't get out of my mind."

"What was it?"

"You know that my little sister Mary is dead—died when ten years old. My mother was a widow, poor, but good. She never seemed like herself afterwards. In a year or so, she died, too; and then I, having no home, and no mother, came to the war. But last night I dreamed the war was over, and I went back to my home, and just before I got to the house, my mother and little sister came out to meet me. I didn't seem to remember they were dead! How glad they were! And how my mother, in her smiles, pressed me to her heart! Oh, sir, it was just as real as you are real now!"

"Thank God, Tom, that you have such a mother, not really dead, but in heaven, and that you are hoping, through Christ, to meet her again." The boy wiped his eyes and was comforted.

The next day there was terrible fighting. Tom's drum was heard all day long, here and there. Four times the ground was swept and occupied by the two contending armies. But as the night came on, both paused, and neither dared to go on the field, lest the foe be there. Tom, "the young deacon," it was known, was wounded and left on the battle-field. His company encamped near the battle-field. In the evening, when the noise of battle was over, and all was still, they heard a voice singing, away off on the field. They felt sure it was Tom's voice. Softly and beautifully the words floated on the wings of night,—

"Jesus! lover of my soul,
Let me to Thy bosom fly,
While the billows near me roll,
While the tempest still is high.
Hide me, O my Saviour, hide,
Till the storm of life is past!
Safe into the haven guide,
Oh, receive my soul at last.

Other refuge have I none,
Hangs my helpless soul on Thee!
Leave, ah! leave me not alone,
Still support and comfort me!"—

The voice stopped here, and there was silence. In the morning the soldiers went out and found Tom sitting on the ground, and leaning against a stump—dead! His soul went up in the song. Did his mother and Mary meet him? Who can say? But poor Tom was not created for this world, was he?—

"ROCK OF AGES, CLEFT FOR ME."

—*Augustus Toplady.*

BELCHER writes:—"The death of the author

of this favorite hymn was indeed that of the Christian. A short time before his decease, at his own request, his physician felt his pulse, and was asked what he thought of it. His reply was that "the heart and arteries beat weaker and weaker;" the reply of the dying saint, as the sweetest of smiles sat on his countenance, was, "Why, that is a good sign my death is fast approaching; and, blessed be God, I can add that my heart beats every day stronger and stronger for glory." Still nearer to his end he said, "Oh, my dear sir, it is impossible to describe how good God is to me! Since I have been sitting in this chair this afternoon, glory be to His name, I have enjoyed such a season, such sweet communion with God, and such delightful manifestations of his presence and love to my soul, that it is impossible for any language to express them. I have had peace and joy unutterable; and I fear not that God's consolations and support will continue." But immediately recollecting himself, he continued, "What have I said? God may, to be sure, as a Sovereign, hide his face and his smiles from me.

However, I believe he will not; and if he should, yet will I trust in him. I know I am safe; for his love and his covenant are everlasting." Within an hour of his death, he said, "It will not be long before God takes me; for no mortal man can live"—bursting, while he said it, into tears of joy, "after the glories which God has manifested to my soul."

DR. POMEROY, in speaking of a visit he made a few years ago to an Armenian Church in Constantinople, says that he was greatly pleased with their singing, though he could not understand the words. They all sung the same part, and while singing the hymns their eyes were closed, and as they sung the tears trickled down over many cheeks.

On inquiry what the hymn was, one of the missionaries told him it was,—

"Rock of Ages, cleft for me!"

O that the singing of these precious words would have like effect on the members of our American churches!

Dr. T. L. Cuyler says of this hymn:—"Of all its lines the two finest are those which are carved on a monument in Greenwood, beneath the figure of Faith kneeling at a cross:

"Nothing in my hands I bring,
Simply to Thy cross I cling."

A LITTLE girl of my acquaintance was once looking at a picture, which represents a rock in the midst of a stormy sea, bearing upon its summit a cross to which a female figure just recovered from the angry waves clings, faint and exhausted, while at her feet a hand, grasping a part of the wreck, is just disappearing in the black water.

"What does that mean," asked the child.

"It is called 'The Rock of Ages,'" was the answer.

"That means Jesus, to whom we cling for salvation."

"You know the hymn says, 'Other refuge have I none.'"

"Oh! yes," said the child, after a moment's hesitation, "but that rock isn't *my* Jesus; when I cling to him he reaches down and clings too."

The following beautiful poem is in itself a commentary on this popular hymn: —

"ROCK OF AGES."

"Rock of Ages, cleft for me,"
  Thoughtlessly the maiden sung,
Fell the words unconsciously
  From her girlish, gleeful tongue;
Sang as little children sing;
  Sang as sing the birds in June;
Fell the words like light leaves down
  On the current of the tune—
"Rock of Ages, cleft for me,
  Let me hide myself in Thee."

"Let me hide myself in Thee,"
  Felt her soul no need to hide;
Sweet the song as song could be—
  And she had no thought beside;
All these words unheedingly
  Fell from lips untouched by care,
Dreaming not that each might be
  On some other lips a prayer—
"Rock of Ages, cleft for me,
  Let me hide myself in Thee."

"Rock of Ages, cleft for me"—
  'Twas a woman sung them now,
Pleadingly and prayerfully;
  Every word her heart did know,
Rose the song as storm-tossed bird
  Beats with weary wing the air,
Every note with sorrow stirred—
  Every syllable a prayer—
"Rock of Ages, cleft for me,
  Let me hide myself in Thee."

"Rock of Ages, cleft for me,"
Lips grown aged sung the hymn
Trustingly and tenderly—
Voice grown weak and eyes grown dim,
"Let me hide myself in Thee,"
Trembling though the voice, and low,
Ran the sweet strain peacefully,
Like a river in its flow.
Sung as only they can sing
Who life's thorny paths have pressed;
Sung as only they can sing
Who behold the promised rest—
"Rock of Ages, cleft for me,
Let me hide myself in Thee."

"Rock of Ages, cleft for me,"
Sung above a coffin-lid;
Underneath, all restfully,
All life's joys and sorrows hid.
Nevermore, O storm-tossed soul!
Nevermore from wind or tide,
Nevermore from billow's roll,
Wilt thou need thyself to hide.
Could the sightless, sunken eyes,
Closed beneath the soft gray hair,
Could the mute and stiffened lips
Move again in pleading prayer,
Still, aye, still, the words would be,
"Let me hide myself in Thee."

"ALL HAIL THE POWER OF JESUS' NAME!"

—*Rev. Edward Perronet.*

ABOUT the year 1808, this grand old hymn

was printed at Canterbury on a card, for the Sunday School, to which is appended the following notice of the author: —"The Rev. Edward Perronet died at Canterbury, January 2d, 1792. His dying words were, 'Glory to God in the height of his divinity! Glory to God in the depth of his humanity! Glory to God in his all-sufficiency! and into his hands I commend my spirit.'"—*Belcher.*

THE late William Dawson, a very plain man, but a highly popular local preacher among the Wesleyan Methodists of England, was, some years since, preaching in London on the offices of Christ. After presenting him as the great teacher and Priest, who made himself an offering for sin, the preacher introduced him as the King of saints. Having shown that he was king in his own right, he proceeded to the coronation. Borrowing his ideas from scenes familiar to his audience, he marshalled the immense procession moving toward the grand temple to place the insignia of royalty upon the King of the Universe. So vividly did the preacher present the scene, that his hearers almost thought they were gazing upon that long line of patriarchs and kings, prophets and apostles, martyrs and confessors of every age and clime, until at length the great temple was filled, and the solemn and imposing ceremony of coronation was about to take place. The audience by this time were wrought up to the highest pitch of excitement; and, while momentarily expecting to hear the anthem peal out from the vast assemblage, the preacher commenced singing,—

"All hail the power of Jesus' name!"

The effect was electrical. The audience started to their feet and sang the hymn with such spirit and feeling as perhaps it was never sang before or since.—*Belcher.*

"THERE IS A FOUNTAIN FILLED WITH BLOOD."

— *William Cowper.*

A NOTORIOUS robber of New York grew weary of his sinful life, and wanted to become a Christian, but almost despaired of being saved. A Christian man talked and prayed with him, but could not give him any encouragement. He then sang the first verse of—

"There is a fountain filled with blood,"

but the poor man said, "there is nothing in that for me." He then sang the second verse,—

"The dying thief rejoiced to see
That fountain in his day;
And there may I, though vile as he,
Wash all my sins away."

"That means *me*," said the penitent robber. Hope sprung up in his heart, and he was soon after happily converted.

A POOR Sabbath scholar has fallen down a hatchway and broken his hip. The doctor says he is internally injured, and that he cannot help him. The boy's teacher is sent for, and is surprised at the greeting he received. "Teacher, you are just in time to hear my great joy; I am going home to Jesus." "I did not know you ever thought about such things, John; how long have you felt so?" "Dear teacher, you never asked me; I have been longing to have you for six months. Now sing my favorite hymn with me, dear teacher." And while they sang the sweet words,—

> "And sinners plunged beneath THAT flood,
> Lose all their guilty stains,"

the messenger came to call the lad Home.

SHORTLY after the visit of Mr. Moody and Mr. Sankey to Scotland, a little boy passed along the streets of Glasgow in the evening singing,

> "There is a fountain filled with blood."

A Christian policeman joined in the song. At the end of the policeman's beat he asked the boy if he understood what he was singing.

"Oh yes, said the little fellow, "*I know it in my heart and it is very precious.*"

A few evenings afterward some one, in conversation with the policeman, said:

"Do you know that a woman standing where we are was awakened and saved by hearing the other night a hymn sung by a policeman and a boy?"

> "E'er since by faith I saw the stream
> Thy flowing wounds supply,
> Redeeming love has been my theme
> And shall be till I die.

"Then in a nobler, sweeter song
 I'll sing thy power to save,
When this poor, lisping, stammering tongue
 Lies silent in the grave."

In a religious awakening a pastor invited a meeting of the young people of his congregation in the parsonage. The room was thronged with anxious inquirers. During the opening exercises he observed a young lady deeply affected. She was one of the most estimable young ladies of his congregation, one whose amenity of manner and purity of life might have been copied to advantage by many of the members of his church. Calling her by name, he inquired, "What has brought *you* here?"

"My sins, sir," was her deep and earnest response.

"But," said he, wishing to test the soundness of her convictions, "what have you done that you should feel so deeply?"

"O, sir," said she, "I hate God, and I know it."

Perhaps never before that hour had she comprehended how deep and fearful is the enmity of the carnal mind to God.

"I hate God, and I know it; I have a heart opposed to all good; I hate my own life, and now see how empty and worthless — nay, how insulting to God — have been all my good deeds, with which I thought to merit his favor! O how utterly wretched and lost is my soul!"

She rose and went into an adjoining room. There she paced the floor to and fro, in an agony of soul bordering upon despair.

"What mockery!" she exclaimed. "How have I deceived and ruined my soul! My condemnation is just! But O, my God, where shall deliverance be found?"

Just then she took a hymn-book, and her eye lit upon this stanza:

> "There is a fountain filled with blood,
> Drawn from Immanuel's veins;
> And sinners, plunged beneath that flood,
> Lose all their guilty stains."

In one moment she was enabled, by faith, to plunge beneath that flood. Quicker than thought light broke in upon her soul; the Divine Spirit filled her with his presence, and she burst forth into an exultant song,—

"My God is reconciled;
His pard'ning voice I hear:
He owns me for his child
I can no longer fear."

At Hamilton Camp-meeting a man, whose vices had made him miserable, stopped at one of the tents where he heard them singing,—

"There is a fountain filled with blood."

He heard the first verse :
"That's not for me."
The second began,—

"The dying thief rejoiced to see
That fountain in his day—"

"That's for me! That's for me! and a few minutes later he was kneeling in the tent praying for mercy, which he soon found.

"OH, FOR A THOUSAND TONGUES TO SING."

—*Charles Wesley.*

Charles Wesley, when speaking to Peter Bohler of the sense of pardon sealed on his conscience, said: "I suppose I had better keep silent about it." The good Moravian shook him by the hand and replied, "Oh! no, my brother; if you had a thousand tongues, go and use them all for Jesus;" and he went home and wrote:—

"Oh, for a thousand tongues to sing
My great Redeemer's praise;
The glories of my God and King,
The triumphs of his grace.

"My gracious Master, and my God,
Assist me to proclaim,—
To spread through all the earth abroad,
The honors of thy name.

"Jesus, the name that charms my fears
That bids our sorrows cease;
'Tis music in the sinner's ears,
'Tis life, and health, and peace.

He breaks the power of cancell'd sin,
He sets the pris'ner free;
His blood can make the foulest clean;
His blood avail'd for me."

THIS hymn is also said to have been written by the author on the first anniversary of the conversion of himself and his brother John. It originally contained eighteen verses, and was entitled "*For the Anniversary of One's*

Conversion." It was first published in the year 1739.

DURING the great conflagration in Chicago, the Grace Methodist Episcopal Church, with many others, was burned. The pastor, Rev. Mr. Parkhurst, after toiling all night with and among the sufferers, pointing them to the many mansions on high, and the temple not made with hands, where no fire shall consume, met three hundred of his homeless people on the ruins of their late beautiful house of worship, and sang:—

"Oh, for a thousand tongues to sing
My great Redeemer's praise."

"NEARER, MY GOD, TO THEE."
—*Sarah Flower Adams.*

DR. CUYLER says of Sarah Flower, the writer of this soul-stirring hymn: "She was worthy of her name. For 'Sarah' signifies a princess, and a sweeter fragrance has rarely exhaled from any flower in the garden of the Lord. This gifted girl married Mr. William

B. Adams, an English civil engineer of superior abilities. She was of frail constitution, and amid many bodily sufferings she kept her pen at work upon various poetical productions. At what time she caught the inspiration to compose that one immortal hymn, which is now sung around the globe, we have never learned. Probably it was some season of peculiar trial, when the bruised spirit emitted the odors of a child-like submission to a chastening Father. It must have oozed from a bleeding heart. Her hymn first appeared in a volume of sacred lyrics, published by a Mr. Fox, in England, about the year 1841. The authoress did not live to catch the echoes of the fame it was to bring, for she died in 1849, at the age of 44. She was buried in Harlow, in Essex, and for several years her name was known to but few beyond the circle of loving friends who read it on her monument. Presently the hymn began to work its way into various collections of songs for worship. It crossed to America. It was heard with delight in our prayer meetings. It was married to the noble tune of "Bethany," and everybody caught the glorious strain. In noonday gatherings for prayer, it soon became so familiar that if any one "struck up" the hymn the whole audience joined in.

"MY FAITH LOOKS UP TO THEE."

—*Ray Palmer, D. D.*

IT is, by far, the most precious contribution which American genius has yet made to the hymnology of the Christian church. The author of it was a native of "Little Compton," in Rhode Island, and was graduated from old Yale in 1830. Immediately after leaving college he came to New York, and spent a few hours each day in teaching young ladies in a school which stood in the then fashionable quarter of Fulton Street, behind St. Paul's church. In December of that year (1830), just forty years ago, he sat down one day in his room, and wrote in his pocket memorandum book four simple verses, which he says "were born of my own soul," and were not written to be seen by another eye. He wrote them rapidly, and with his eyes swimming in tears. The first verse reads thus: —

"My faith looks up to Thee,
Thou Lamb of Calvary,
Saviour divine!
Now hear me while I pray,
Take all my guilt away,
Oh, let me from this day
Be wholly thine!"

He put the memorandum book into his pocket, and carried it there for two whole years, little dreaming that he was carrying about with him his own passport to immortality. One day Dr. Lowell Mason met him in the streets of Boston, and asked him to furnish some hymns for the volume of "Spiritual Songs," which he (Dr. Mason) and Dr. Thomas Hastings were about to publish. The young college graduate drew from his pocket the lines,—

"My faith looks up to Thee."

Dr. Mason went home, and catching a similar inspiration to that of the author of the lines, composed for them that beautiful tune of "Olivet," to which the hymn is wedded unto this day. Dr. Mason met the author a few days afterwards and said to him prophetically, "Mr. Palmer, you may live many years and do many good things, but I think that you will be best known to posterity as the author of this hymn." The prediction is fulfilled. The man who sang this sweet song of Calvary is still living, and has composed many tender and beautiful poems and discourses; but his devout mind flowered out in one matchless lily whose rich odors have filled the Courts of our God with fragrance.

How many a penitent, while reading or singing that hymn, has looked up to Calvary's Cross and found peace in believing! In how many a prayer-meeting has it been sung through tears of holy gratitude! To how many a sick chamber and dying bed has it come like a strain from that heavenly land which was already in full view!

The poetry of the hymn is as perfect as its theology. In its structure it closely resembles the "Rock of Ages." It begins in penitence; it ends in praise. It begins in heart-broken sorrow, and concludes with the most glorious assurance of hope. In the first verse the suppliant is represented as bowing before the crucified Saviour, and looking up to him, and to him only. He sees none but Jesus. His cry is,—

> "Take all my guilt away."

His aspiration is,—

> "Oh, let me from this day
> Be wholly thine."

Before that cross the praying soul obtains strength, and a pure, warm, and changeless love for his Redeemer. He is filled with a "living fire." He is the new man in Christ Jesus. But as he looks forward, he foresees a "dark maze" of trial before him, overhung with clouds of grief that lower black and terrible, and sometimes weep great showers of tears. Surrounded with these discouraging clouds of confusion and temptation he shouts out like one lost in the dark,—

> "Be thou my guide,
> Bid darkness turn to day,
> Wipe sorrow's tear away,
> Nor let me ever stray
> From Thee aside."

Before him lies still one more valley darker

than any passed before. It is that vale in which end's "life's transient dream." Through it rolls death's cold and sullen stream. He already imagines himself in the swelling of Jordan. And as the floods go over him, he lifts his last victorious voice of sublime trust,—

"Blest Saviour! then in love
Fear and distrust remove;
Oh, bear me safe above,
A ransomed soul."

Such is the grandeur of American hymns. Is it not the graudeur of this century? And if our readers wish to know, and to thank its modern author, they have but to go into "the Bible House" in New York, and take by the hand our genial and beloved friend, Dr. Ray Palmer.—*Rev. T. L. Cuyler in "Heart Life."*

"HAVE YOU ON THE LORD BELIEVED?"

A VAST fortune was left in the hands of a minister for one of his poor parishioners. Fearing that it might be squandered, if suddenly bestowed upon him, the wise minister sent him a little at a time with a note saying: "*This is thine: use it wisely; there is more to follow.*"

This incident, as told by Mr. Moody, suggested to Mr. Bliss his popular hymn, "More to follow."

"Have you on the Lord believed?
  Still there's more to follow;
Of his grace have you received?
  Still there's more to follow;
Oh, the grace the Father shows!
  Still there's more to follow,
Freely he his grace bestows,
  Still there's more to follow."

"THERE WERE NINETY AND NINE."

VARIOUS statements having been published respecting the origin of the famous hymn, "The Ninety and Nine," sung by Mr. Sankey, it is well to follow them with the sweet singer's own account, which is to the effect that the hymn was written by a Miss Eliza C. Clephane of Melrose, Scotland, a member of the church of Scotland. It was first published in *The Family Treasury*, of which the late Dr. Arnot was editor. But Mr. Sankey found it in *The Christian Age*, a London religious paper.

"There were ninety and nine that safely lay
  In the shelter of the fold,
But one was out on the hills away,
  Far off from the gates of gold—

Away on the mountains wild and bare,
 Away from the tender Shepherd's care.

"'Lord, thou hast here thy ninety and nine;
 Are they not enough for thee?'
But the Shepherd made answer: ''Tis of mine
 Has wandered away from me;
And although the road be rough and steep
I go to the desert to find my sheep."

"DEPTHS OF MERCY! CAN THERE BE."

— *Charles Wesley.*

AN actress in one of the English provincial or country theatres, was one day passing through the streets of the town in which she resided, when her attention was attracted by the sound of voices in a poor cottage before her. Curiosity prompted her to look in at the open door, when she saw a few people sitting together, one of whom, at the moment of her observation, was giving out the hymn, which the others joined in singing,—

"Depths of mercy! can there be
Mercy still reserved for me?"

The tune was sweet and simple; but she heeded it not. The words had riveted her attention, and she stood motionless, until she was invited to enter by the woman of the house, who had observed her standing at the door. She remained during a prayer which was offered up by one of the little company; and, uncouth as the expressions sounded, perhaps, to her ears, they carried with them a conviction of sincerity on the part of the person engaged. She quitted the cottage; but the words of the hymn followed her, and at last she resolved to procure the book which contained it. She did so; and the more she read it, the more decided her serious impressions became. She attended the ministry of the gospel, read her hitherto neglected and despised Bible, and bowed herself in humility and contrition of heart before Him whose mercy she now felt she needed, whose sacrifices are those of a broken heart and a contrite spirit, and who has declared that with such sacrifices he is well pleased.

Her profession she determined at once to renounce, and for some time excused herself from appearing on the stage, without, however, making known her resolution finally to leave it.

The manager of the theatre called upon

her one morning and requested her to sustain the principal character in a new play which was to be performed the next week. She had frequently performed this character to general admiration; but she now, however, told him her resolution never to appear as an actress again, at the same time giving her reasons. At first he attempted to overcome her scruples by ridicule; but this was unavailing: he then represented the loss he would incur by her refusal, and concluded by promising that if, to oblige him, she would act on this occasion, it would be the last request of the kind he would ever make. Unable to resist his solicitations, she promised to appear, and on the appointed evening went to the theatre. The character which she assumed required her, on her first entrance, to sing a song; and, when the curtain drew up, the orchestra immediately began the accompaniment. But she stood as if lost in thought, and as one forgetting all around her and her situation. The music ceased, but she did not sing; and, supposing her to be overcome by embarrassment, the band again commenced.

A second time they paused for her to begin; and still she did not open her lips. A third time the air was played; and then, with clasped hands and eyes suffused with tears, she sang,—not the words of the song, but,—

"Depth of mercy! can there be
Mercy still reserved for me?"

It is almost needless to add that the performance was suddenly ended. Many ridiculed, though some were induced from that memorable night to "consider their ways," and to reflect on the wonderful power of the religion which could influence the heart and change the life of one hitherto so vain and so evidently pursuing the road which leadeth to destruction. The change in Miss —— was as permanent as it was singular: she walked consistently with her profession of religion for many years, and at length became the wife of a minister of the gospel of our Lord Jesus Christ.—*Belcher; see also "Hedged in," by E. S. Phelps, p.* 35.

"FREE FROM THE LAW, OH, HAPPY CONDITION."

A GENTLEMAN in Edinburgh was in distress of soul, and happened to linger in a pew after the noon meeting. The choir had remained to practise, and began

"Free from the law, oh, happy condition,"

etc. Quickly the Spirit of God carried that truth home to the awakened conscience, and he was at rest in the finished work of Jesus.

"GUIDE ME, O THOU GREAT JEHOVAH."

—*William Williams.*

THE power of this hymn as a shield is illustrated by an allegory of Christmas Evans. "I see the unclean spirit rising like a winged dragon, circling in the air, and seeking for a resting-place. Casting his fiery glances toward a certain neighborhood, he spies a young man in the bloom of life, and rejoicing in his strength, seated on the front of his cart, going for lime. 'There he is!' said the old dragon; 'his veins are full of blood, and his bones of marrow; I will throw into his bosom sparks from hell; I will set all his passions on fire; I will lead him from bad to worse, until he shall perpetrate every sin. I will make him a murderer, and his soul shall sink, never again to rise, in the lake of fire.' By this time, I see it descend, with a fell swoop toward the earth; but, nearer the youth, the dragon heard him sing,—

'Guide me, O Thou Great Jehovah!
Pilgrim through this barren land:
I am weak, but thou art mighty;
Hold me with thy powerful hand.
Strong Deliverer,
Be thou still my strength and shield.'

'A dry, dry place this,' says the old dragon; and away he goes. But I see him again hovering about in the air, and casting about for a suitable resting-place. Beneath his eye there is a flowery meadow, watered by a crystal stream; and he descries among the kine a maiden, about eighteen years of age, picking up here and there a beautiful flower. 'There she is!' says Apollyon, intent upon her soul; 'I will poison her thoughts; she shall stray from the paths of virtue; she shall think evil thoughts and become impure; she shall become a lost creature in the great city, and, at last, I will cast her down from the precipice into everlasting burnings.' Again he took his downward flight, but he no sooner came near the maiden, than he heard her sing the following words, with a voice that might have melted the rocks,—

'Other refuge have I none;
Hangs my helpless soul on thee;
Leave, ah! leave me not alone:
Still support and comfort me.'

Again he turned away defeated. The devil, can say, as did the enemies of the reformers, 'By their songs we are conquered.'"

OUR SHIELD OF SONG.

"ALMOST PERSUADED."

MR. SANKEY was with Mr. Moody in Philadelphia, years since, during the progress of a very interesting meeting at Dr. Reed's church, when many were being awakened, and sang this beautiful Gospel hymn, "Almost Persuaded." After the close of the meeting, an attorney, who had been very much interested, came forward and said that he was not only "almost" but "altogether persuaded" to put his trust in the Lord Jesus. This sweet song was used of the Holy Ghost in carrying the blessed Gospel of God's Son to his heart.

"Almost persuaded" now to believe;
"Almost persuaded" Christ to receive;
Seems now some soul to say,
"Go, Spirit, go thy way,
Some more convenient day
On thee I'll call."

"Almost persuaded," come, come to-day;
"Almost persuaded," turn not away;
Jesus invites you here,
Angels are lingering near,
Prayers rise from hearts so dear:
O wanderer, come.

"Almost persuaded," harvest is past!
"Almost persuaded," doom comes at last!

"Almost" cannot avail;
"Almost" is but to fail!
Sad, sad that bitter wail —
"Almost — *but lost!*"

"THERE IS A LAND OF PURE DELIGHT."

—*Isaac Watts.*

WE learn from an American writer, who obtained his information on the spot, that the author of this familiar hymn, — in which every image is said to be scriptural, every suggestion appropriate, and every association holy, — wrote it at Southampton, his native town, while sitting at the window of a parlor which overlooked the River Itchen, and in full view of the Isle of Wight, "beyond the swelling flood," representing "the land of pure delight,"—

"Where everlasting spring abides,
And never-withering flowers."

It is indeed a fair and beautiful type of that paradise of which the poet sung. It rises from the margin of the flood and swells into boundless prospect, all mantled in the richest verdure of summer, checkered with forest growth, and fruitful fields under the highest cultivation, and gardens, and villas, and every adornment which the hand of man, in the series of ages, could create on such susceptible grounds. As the poet looked upon the waters then before him, he thought of the final passage of the Christian,—

> "Death, like a narrow sea, divides
> This heavenly land from ours."

—*Belcher.*

OH, I do not know how we shall stand the first day in heaven. Do you not think we will break down in the song from over-delight? I once gave out in church the hymn:

> "There is a land of pure delight,
> Where saints immortal reign,"

and an aged man standing in front of the pulpit sang heartily the first verse, and then he sat down weeping. I said to him afterward, "Father Linton, what made you cry over that hymn?" He said, "I could not stand it — the joys that are coming."

—*T. Dewitt Talmage.*

"ARISE, MY SOUL, ARISE."
—*Charles Wesley.*

"NOTICE the first trial that the world ever saw. God reads the charge, 'Where is Abel, thy brother?" Cain has the presumption to deny his guilt: 'I know not.' The trial proceeds: *a brother's blood* is the terrible accuser, and when sentence of banishment has been pronounced, the condemned man goes forth, crying out, 'My guilt is greater than I can bear.' 'From thy face shall I be hid.'"

"I am thinking of another trial scene," said Mizpah, with such emotion that every one eagerly listened. "The judge is the infinite God, and the guilty one is my soul. The blood of Christ might cry out against me from the cross, as my accuser, but it 'speaketh *better things* than that of Abel;' it speaketh as my advocate,—

'Five bleeding wounds he bears,
Received on Calvary;
They pour effectual prayers,
They strongly plead for me:

NOTE.—This hymn represents every step of the prodigal's experience, from the time when he says "I will *arise*," to the glad moment when the Father "owns him for his child." The story in Luke xv. should be read in connection with the hymn.

Forgive him, O forgive, they cry,
Nor let that ransomed sinner die.'

Through this advocate we may be saved from the terrible cry of banishment, 'From thy face shall I be hid!'"

"STAND UP! STAND UP FOR JESUS!"

—*Rev. Geo. Duffield, Jr.*

THIS deservedly popular hymn was composed to be sung after a sermon delivered by its author, the Sabbath following the mournfully sudden death of the Rev. Dudley A. Tyng, who was called from earth in 1858, and whose dying counsel to his brethren in the ministry was,—

"Stand up for Jesus!"

—*Belcher.*

"COME THOU FOUNT OF EVERY BLESSING."

—*Robinson.*

THE author of this hymn was at different times Calvinist, Socinian, Baptist, Independent, Methodist and lastly irreligious. During this last state of life his attention was called to this hymn, and he said, "I would give a thousand worlds to enjoy the feelings I then had." In view of such an experience we may well pray, as well as sing,—

> "Let thy goodness, like a fetter,
> Bind my wandering heart to thee."

"JUST AS I AM, WITHOUT ONE PLEA."

A JEW in New York, who professed not to believe in either Judaism or Christianity, a worldly, fashionable, pleasure-serving, man was seized by a dangerous disease and told that he could live only a few days.

In spite of professed infidelity he became anxious about the future. Minister after minister called upon him, talked and prayed, but in vain. At length a Christian business man came in, and during his call sang,—

> "Just as I am without one plea,"

The Jew exclaimed, "Do you really mean that for me? You know what I have been — worldly, skeptical, pleasure-loving. Be very sure, now. Do you really mean that for me?"

"Yes, I do just that." With much inward struggle the Jew was able to make the words of the hymn his own and say to Christ,—

> "Just as I am, I come, I come."

A few days later he died trusting in Him,—

> "Whose love unknown
> Had broken every barrier down."

A LITTLE boy came to one of our city missionaries, and holding out a dirty and well-worn bit of printed paper, said,—

"Please, sir, father sent me to get a clean paper like that."

Taking it from his hand, the missionary unfolded it, and found it was a page containing that beautiful hymn of which the first stanza is as follows:

> "Just as I am, without one plea
> But that thy blood was shed for me,
> And that thou biddst me come to thee,
> O Lamb of God, I come!"

The missionary looked down with interest into the face earnestly upturned to him, and asked the little boy where he got it, and why he wanted a clean one.

"We found it, sir," said he, "in sister's pocket after she died; and she used to sing it all the time when she was sick, and loved it so much that father wanted to get a clean one to put in a frame to hang it up. Wont you give us a clean one, sir?"

This little page, with a single hymn on it, had been cast upon the air, like a fallen leaf, by Christian hands, humbly hoping to do some possible good. In some little mission Sunday-school, probably, this poor girl had thoughtlessly received it, afterwards to find in it, we hope, the Gospel of her salvation. Could she, in any probability, have gone down into death, sweetly singing that hymn of penitence and faith in Jesus to her latest breath, without the saving knowledge of him, which the Holy Spirit imparts?

"PRAISE GOD FROM WHOM ALL BLESSINGS FLOW."

MANY have heard from Chaplain McCabe's own fire-touched lips, how this grand old doxology, that has doubtless been on more lips than any other uninspired production, was sung by the starving "boys in blue" that were incarcerated in Libby Prison. Day after day they saw comrades passing away, and their numbers increased by fresh, living recruits for the grave. One night about ten o'clock, through the stillness and the darkness, they heard the tramp of coming feet, that soon stopped before the prison door until arrangements could be made inside. In the company was a young Baptist minister, whose heart almost fainted as he looked on those cold walls and thought of the suffering inside. Tired and weary he sat down, put his face in his hands and wept. Just then a lone voice of deep, sweet pathos, sung out from an upper window,—

"Praise God from whom all blessings flow;"

and a dozen manly voices joined in the second line,—

"Praise Him all creatures here below;"

and then by the time the third was reached, more than a score of hearts were full, and these joined to send the words on high,—

"Praise Him above ye heavenly host;"

and by this time the prison was all alive,

and seemed to quiver with the sacred song, as from every room and cell those brave men sang,—

> "Praise Father, Son, and Holy Ghost."

As the song died out on the still night that enveloped in darkness the doomed city of Richmond, the young man arose and happily said,—

> "Prisons would palaces prove,
> If Jesus would dwell with me there."

In the great cotton famine in England, which desolated Lancashire for long and weary months, the conduct of the operatives was the admiration of the world. There were no riots and no excess of crimes. The people, men and women, went into the Sunday-school houses and prayed. They had been taught to do so, and they were upheld in the time of trial by the truths they had learned. When the first wagon load of cotton arrived, the people unhooked the horses and drew it themselves, and surrounding it began to sing — what do you think they sang? They sang the grand old doxology, while the tears came flowing down their cheeks.

CONSECRATED VOICES.

A YOUNG Scottish lady of rank, whose heart the Lord had touched and opened, longed to draw others within the circle of a Saviour's love; but among the gay and proud who were her companions, the merry jest, the gay laugh, and the light and frivolous manner of her associates, hindered every effort, and seemed to hedge her way before her on every hand. Discouraged and sad, oppressed with the burden of the Lord, and knowing not how to attain the desire of her heart, she carried the matter to God in prayer, and, as was her custom, closed the day with a song of praise. Shortly after she had finished her song, her serving maid entered the room in tears, and besought her to sing again the sacred words, and in broken accents told how those strains had touched and melted her heart.

"No words of entreaty," said she, "could ever affect my soul as those plaintive songs to which for weeks I had listened, as my mistress poured out in them her love for the Redeemer, and her faith and trust in him."

Sleep fled that night from the eyes of the young disciple, in the new joy and thankfulness that filled her heart at the discovery of the blessing God had granted upon the songs she had sung. "That talent," she said, "I have consecrated to God. I will sing for him; and if through this means I may touch souls, my happiness shall be complete."

From this time, she devoted herself to the study and expression of sacred song; and while she touched with skill the various instruments on which she had learned to play, her voice of wondrous power would entrance and thrill her hearers. It was the outgushing of her joyous heart; the thanksgiving of a redeemed soul; her testimony, poured upon careless ears, concerning the wondrous love of him who came to save our race; who cares for all his creatures; who gathered little children to his arms, and whose blessing crowns with joy the saint of God, even down to hoary hairs. Many were charmed and cheered with her songs. The sweet story of old, thus rendered, seemed to possess new power to melt the careless heart. In cottages and halls, in the drawing-room of wealth and the homes of humble life, she sung her songs for Jesus, while with lifted heart she sought his blessing on the offering; and ere many months had passed away, she had the delight of knowing that numbers of those around her had, through the songs she sang, been led to taste the joy which she tasted, being brought up out of the horrible pit and miry clay, and placed upon the Living Rock, and having a new song put in their mouths.

THE choir of a church in New York city have truly consecrated their gift of song to the service of Christ. Not content with leading the praise of the great congregation, they are earnest song-workers in the Sunday-school. And they do not stop here. An aged blind woman will tell you how often they make her lonely home happy, bringing to her visions and dreams of the beautiful land. No wonder the dear old soul, in humble, but heartfelt appreciation, breaks in upon the strains which they sing, with her tender, "Bless the Lord!" If you follow these song messengers after they have left the blind Christian, you shall find them among the sick and dying. The sufferer forgets his pain, in listening to their melodies; and the spirit that is going home, floats peacefully away to its rest in heaven.

Church and Sunday-school singers everywhere might well ponder the blessed example of this choir, and join them in making the waste places around them vocal with "songs of the beautiful."

APPENDIX.

BIOGRAPHICAL SKETCH OF MR. IRA D. SANKEY.

MR. SANKEY was born in Edinburgh, Pa., in the year 1840. His father was English, and his mother Scotch-Irish. The early influences that surrounded his life were those of a Christian home. A Scotch neighbor named Frazer introduced him to the Sunday-school at an early age, and by this and other acts of Christian friendship greatly endeared himself to the future evangelist, who often makes grateful mention of his kindness, and his praying as the means of his conversion. At seventeen Mr. Sankey joined the Methodist Episcopal church, of which he is still a member.

When only twenty he was elected superintendent in the Sunday-school and while filling this position began to sing sacred solos and to use sacred songs to express and impress the Gospel. A few years later he was appointed a class-leader, and in that position urged upon his class the importance of using God's "testimonies" in their testimonies, quoting much from the Bible.

During the war he served his country as a soldier, and after it was over, became President of the Young Men's Christian Association at Newcastle, Pa., which was then his home. While filling this position Mr. Moody met him at a Young Men's Christian Association Convention, and, being greatly impressed by his way of singing sacred songs, earnestly invited him to come to Chicago to "sing the Gospel" there as an evangelistic work. After prayerful consideration of the matter Mr. Sankey gave up his business and entered upon the evangelistic labors in which he has been so useful since that time.

Not long after Mr. Sankey began his work in Chicago, Mr. Moody's church with which he was laboring, was burned. The people, however, were held together by Mr. Sankey's earnest efforts joined with those of Mr. Moody.

It was at this time that Mr. Sankey received

his greatest incentive to his Christian work through the conversion of a child by the influence of the song,—

"Jesus loves even me."

at one of his singing meetings in the temporary tabernacle. The incident is given in another place among those connected with the song above mentioned.

Soon after the fire Mr. Sankey went with Mr. Moody to England for evangelistic work. The blessing which attended Mr. Sankey's singing is sufficiently noted in the introductory letter to this volume by Mr. Pentecost, who was himself amid the scenes he describes. The *Daily Edinburgh Review* gave the following editorial in regard to the power of sacred song as Mr. Sankey used it in Scotland:

"The power of music over the mind and soul has been described and illustrated with encyclopædic fullness. Fletcher, of Saltoun, put it in a forcible aphorism which will never be forgotten: 'Let me make the songs of a country, and let who will make the laws.' Wharton boasted that he had overturned an ancient dynasty by a song — the famous Lillibulero. Whitefield protested that it was not to be borne that the devil should have all the best tunes. Luther promoted the Reformation as much by his favorite psalms and hymns as by his preaching; and our own Scottish forefathers made a notable, if not altogether successful attempt to wean the population from the ribald ballads of the sixteenth century, by substituting 'gude and godly ballats,' to the same melodies, and, as far as might be, adopting the same words.

"Yet we have hardly wakened up in Scotland to a sense of the importance of sacred music, notwithstanding all the efforts made during the past twenty or thirty years. In a good many Presbyterian congregations the psalmody is still treated as a bit of convenient padding to be laid between the more important exercises of worship. The minister gives out four verses, sometimes only three, and sometimes only two; and by getting up to preach or to pray, or by looking up his text or his MSS during the singing, shows that he has not got his mind in that part of the proceedings. And should the sermon be of more than the average duration, an attempt is made to recover the lost time by shortening the singing. Any prejudice there may be against 'singing the Gospel' will thaw and resolve itself into a pleasant dew as soon as he opens his mouth.

"Why should there be any prejudice? For generations most of the Highland ministers, and some of the Lowland ministers, too, have sung the Gospel — sung their sermons, aye, and sung their prayers, too. The only difference is that they sing very badly, and Mr. Sankey very beautifully. He accompanied himself on the 'American Organ,' it is true, and some of us who belong to the old school can't swallow the 'kist of whustles' yet. It may help us over this stumbling-block if we consider that with the finest voice and ear in the world nobody could maintain the proper pitch of a melody, singing so long as Mr. Sankey does. And then the American Organ is 'only a little one.' When a deputation from the session waited on Ralph Erskine, to remonstrate with him on the enormity of fiddling, he gave them a beautiful tune on the violincello, and they were so charmed that they returned to their constituents with the report that it was all right — 'it wasna' the wee sinfu' fiddle' that their minister operated upon, but a grand instrument, full of grave sweet melody. I'm afraid some good, true blue Presbyterians will be excusing Mr. Sankey's organ, and themselves for listening to it, by some such plea as that."

After "singing the Gospel" in many of the largest cities of England, Scotland and Ireland, Mr. Sankey has returned to our own country again, and has achieved "song victories" on our own shores equal to those which God awarded to him in other lands. We shall close this brief sketch of a career which we trust will long continue, by quoting an editorial from "*The Inter-Ocean*" of Chicago in regard to "Mr. Sankey's Musical Oratory":

"People are not agreed as to what rank Mr. Sankey shall take as a singer, but they are agreed as to the point that he is just the man to join Mr. Moody in his great work. The methods of the two men are dissimilar, and they appear on the platform in marked contrast. Mr. Moody seizes a crowd at any moment, whether it be noisy or quiet, and asserts his authority.

"He never stands on ceremony, but grapples with the giant at once, and with a supreme consciousness that he will not lose his grip proceeds to the business in hand. Mr. Sankey, on the other hand, approaches a great crowd with almost womanly gentleness. He touches the keys of the organ with soft reverence. He waits till the Tabernacle is so quiet that you can hear a pin drop; he leans forward to say a few words in an appealing, musical tone, as though he wanted to be sure that the people were all in responsive mood, and then he takes possession and carries the crowd with him. His singing is a sort of musical oratory, and it affects or influences people as an oratorical performance rather than a musical one. That is to say, Mr. Sankey touches the same chords, arouses the same feelings, appeals to the same emotions that would be struck or aroused by a persuasive speaker, and he sways an audience precisely as it would be surged by a man of rare eloquence.

"If there be arts in his manner, they are of the orator, rather than of the musician. His sentences come to the audience clean cut and ringing with melody. The sentiment lives in the lines and in the tone as well as in the music. He sings as one in earnest, as one whose heart is full of the sentiment of his song, as one anxious to express all the tenderest and liveliest feelings of the human heart.

"Mr. Moody steps on the platform like a blacksmith approaching his forge. He makes no concessions to circumstances, and is not influenced by unfavorable conditions.

"Mr. Sankey, on the contrary, commences work when the doors are closed. He understands his mission as well as Mr. Moody understands his, and so works with the same great results. He has studied men and women to good purpose, and in choice of subject, in manner of introduction, and style of execution he shows the results of this study. Musicians may not be charmed; he is not singing so much for them as for the men and women with troubled hearts; for men and women perplexed and tired; for men and women who have hearts and heart-aches, as well as ears. He sings now for the mother, now for the father, and again for all. He never makes a mistake. He never promises more than he accomplishes. He never ventures to approach a crowd until it is in the right mood, and he never leaves it until every heart is throbbing responsively. In studying Mr. Moody we are driven forward to the contemplation of the results of his work. In studying Mr. Sankey, we linger over the sweet voice, the trembling tones, the tender words. Mr. Moody startles us and arouses us, while Mr. Sankey soothes and comforts. Mr. Moody, earnest as he is, succeeds without the grace of voice and manner. Mr. Sankey, earnest as he is, succeeds because of grace in voice and manner. He is well fitted to be Mr. Moody's companion, and those who hear him do not wonder at his continued success in this peculiar field."

SAFE WITH THE MASTER.

Where is now our loved one?
  Where, O where?
Not where the living weary,
Not where the dying moan;
Not where the day is dreary,
Not where the night is lone.
Not in a home of weeping,
Not in a darkened room,
Not in a graveyard sleeping
Not in a silent tomb.

Where is now our loved one?
  Where, O where?
Safe in a land immortal,
Safe in a country rare,
Safe in a heavenly portal
Safe in a mansion fair.
Safe with the joys supernal,
Safe with the blest to bow,
Safe with the Love Eternal,
Safe with the Master now.

BY P. P. BLISS.

From "The Prize." Copyrighted.

BIOGRAPHICAL SKETCH OF P. P. BLISS.

BY. MRS. W. F. CRAFTS.

[*Sara J. Timanus.*]

FRIDAY, Dec. 29, 1876, was the last day that dawned upon the earthly life of "The sweet singer of Israel," P. P. Bliss. On the day previous Mr. Bliss and his wife left their mother's home, Rome, Pa., where they had been making a Christmas visit, and started for Chicago, when Mr. Bliss and Major D. W. Whittle were to continue, in the great Tabernacle, the evangelistic work begun by Moody and Sankey. As he rode he busied himself with Bible and paper, composing a new song which perished with him.

When within about twelve hours ride of Chicago, the train on which they were traveling was wrecked by the fearful "Ashtabula disaster," words that will ring like a funeral knell in many lives for years to come. By the giving way of the bridge which spanned the Ashtabula River the whole train was precipicated into the ice-bound stream below. The cars were soon in flames, and the devastating elements of fire and water, adding their fury to the wild storm that was raging at the time, rendered the scene one of untold horror. The only circumstance connected with the death of Mr. and Mrs. Bliss that can be ascertained is that Mr. Bliss, after escaping out of a window of a car was burned to death on going back to rescue his wife.

At the meeting held in memory of Mr. Bliss in Chicago on the following Sunday, the fact was recalled with a sad interest that the last time he had sung in the Moody and Sankey meetings he had said, "I don't know as I shall ever sing here again, but I want to sing this as the language of my heart," and then had sung that song of his:

"I know not the hour my Lord will come
To take me away to his own dear home,
But I know that his presence will lighten the gloom,
And that will be glory for me."

At the time of his death Mr. Bliss was in the

very prime and vigor of manhood, being thirty-eight years of age.

His boyhood and early manhood were spent in northwest Pennsylvania.

In the year 1868, Mr. George F. Root of Chicago, the well-known music publisher, learning of his musical ability — both as a composer and leader, engaged his services. Mr. Bliss then removed to Chicago, and for nearly six years went out into different parts of the West to conduct Normal Musical Institutes. He was also engaged during this time in composing Sunday-school music, the first of which appeared in 1870 in a book edited and published by Mr. George F. Root, entitled, "The Prize."

These were days of beginnings and of trials in the life of Mr. Bliss and his wife. Yet they styled their humble home "The Kot o' Kontent" and gave a cheery welcome to the friends who visited them.

In 1871 Mr. Bliss' first book, "The Charm," appeared and at once gave him a place among the favorite composers of Sunday-school music. About this time he was elected to the position of chorister in the First Congregational Church of Chicago (Rev. Dr. Goodwin's), of which he had become a member. On coming to Chicago, having previously been a Methodist. He was also chosen superintendent of the large Sunday-school of that church, very many of whose members were led to Christ by his influence. Frequent demands were now made upon him to sing at dedications, anniversaries and Sunday-school gatherings. On these occasions he *gave* his services whenever time would permit. His Normal Musical work still continued and in 1872 he published a collection of new songs, duets, trios and quartets, entitled "The Song Tree." The design of the book is beautifully expressed in the following acrostic preface:

"Sing away dreariness,
Tree of my love;
Oh, and to weariness
Rest may'st thou prove:
Nobly endeaver the
Erring to win
Guarding forever from
Evil and sin."

Subsequently appeared "Sunshine," a book for Sunday-schools and "The Joy," for classes, choirs and conventions.

Mr. Bliss at length resigned his position as chorister and his work as a musical leader, with much pecuniary sacrifice, in order to give himself wholly to evangelistic work. In a letter to a friend dated "May 13, 1874," when he was just starting to a Musical Institute, he says:

"Do you know Brother Moody, Whittle, and others are after me to sing Gospel hymns in evangelistic work. Shall I? Where can I accomplish most? Pray that I may make no mistake."

He decided to go into this work, and two months later wrote to the same friend:

"Major Whittle and I are holding protracted meetings. God is wonderfully using us in every way. Help us to praise him for it. I am preparing a book of "Gospel Songs" for our special use, and would be right glad to have you send a list of hymns and tunes which have been most successful in your experience. And above all, pray for the book. All the good in the book must come from God."

This book, "Gospel Songs," was published in 1874 with the following acrostic preface which truly represents its deep spiritual purpose:

"God so loved the world that he gave his
Only begotten
Son, that whosoever believeth on him should not
Perish, but have
Everlasting
Life."

"Serve the Lord with gladness; come before his presence with thanksgiving.
O Lord, open thou my lips and my mouth shall show forth thy praise.
Not unto us, O Lord, not unto us, but unto thy name, give glory.
Great is the Lord, and greatly to be praised.
Sing unto the Lord, bless his name, show forth his salvation from day to day.

Since July 1774 Mr. Bliss has been engaged earnestly and almost constantly in evangelistic work in connection with Major Whittle. The following slip which has sometimes been distributed as an invitation to their meetings shows how they shared the work:

WEEK OF PRAYER

MAJOR WHITTLE

WILL PREACH THE GOSPEL,

AND

P. P. BLISS

WILL SING THE GOSPEL,

this Wednesday Evening, Jan. 6th,

AT UNION PARK CONGREGATIONAL CHURCH,

ASHLAND AVENUE, OPPOSITE PARK.

SEATS FREE. ALL INVITED.

FURTHER APPOINTMENT.

"He hath appointed a day in the which He will judge the world in righteousness by that Man (Jesus Christ) whom He hath ordained; whereof He hath given assurance unto all men in that He hath raised Him from the dead."—Acts. 17: 31.

Friend, are you ready to meet this appointment? There can be no postponement.

Mr. Bliss held these evangelistic meetings in company with Major Whittle, at Mobile, Atlanta, Nashville, Louisville, Chicago, Peoria, Kalamazoo, Jackson, and many other places, and always with great success.

Mr. Bliss sang as earnest ministers preach, not for artistic effects but *to express and impress the Gospel.* In his singing he was putting in practice what he so often exhorted upon others in his song:

> "Let the lower lights be burning,
> Send a gleam across the wave;
> Some poor fainting, struggling seaman
> You may rescue, you may save."

His songs in these "Gospel meetings" were frequently prefaced with a short and earnest prayer by himself or by the reading or repeating of Scripture passages in the audience.

The following brief remarks, made by Mr. Bliss at "The Sunday-school Parliament," on Wellesley Island in the St. Lawrence River, during the summer of 1876, shows his high estimate of sacred music:

"That which ought to have the greatest emphasis just now in regard to sacred music is the need of greater reverence. While a song is being sung, people will pass up a church aisle or a Sunday-school aisle, whisper to each other, move about the room, distribute or collect library books, put on overcoats, or do a score of other *things that one would never think of doing during any other kind of prayer.* When we are offering praise or prayer to God in metre, as much as if we were doing it upon our knees, a reverence of manner and spirit should accompany it. Another thing to be enforced in connection with singing is a greater thoughtfulness in regard to the meaning of what we sing. Are the words prayer? Or praise? Let appropriate *thought* as well as appropriate melody accompany the words."

Mr. Bliss is known even more widely as a composer of sacred song than as a singer, being the author of both words and music of the following popular songs: "Jesus loves even me," "Almost persuaded," "Hold the fort," "Pull for the shore," "What shall the harvest be?" "More to follow," "Hallelujah, 'tis done," "Free from the law," "Let the lower lights be burning," "Whosoever heareth," and "Only an armor-bearer."

In all these and his other hymns Mr. Bliss showed a remarkable skill in versifying evangelical doctrine in the very phrases of Scripture.

Mr. Bliss composed with the greatest ease and his music was mostly bright and cheerful. When Haydn was asked, "why his music was so gladsome," he replied, "I can't make any other. I write as I feel. When I think of God my heart is so full of joy that the words dance and leap from my pen." The same might he said of Mr. Bliss and his music, for he was in perfect harmony with God and his work.

The titles of his books "Sunshine" and "Joy" epitomize the author as a Christian and a composer. Indeed his own name, "Bliss" would fulfill George MacDonald's idea of a true name when he says :

"A name of the ordinary kind in this world has nothing essential in it. It is but a label by which a man and a scrap of history may be known from another man and his scrap of history. The true name is one which expresses the character, the nature, the being, the meaning of the person who bears it. To whom is this name given? 'To him that overcometh.'"

No element of pride entered into Mr. Bliss' estimate of his work. A friend wrote him a letter quoting somewhat from "Waiting and watching for me." The reply came back, "No, I don't seem to rest much in the hope of seeing a throng of heavenly ones waiting and watching for me. They might be in better business. Nor of hearing echoes of my songs there. I want something better. The best things about heaven, seems to me, will be eternal freedom from sin, and Jesus' immediate presence.

'There we shall see His face
And never, never sin.'"

His prayer in song expresses the humility and also the spiritual aspiration of his heart:

"More purity give me,
More strength to o'ercome,
More freedom from earth-stains,
More longings for home;
More fit for the kingdom,
More used would I be,
More blessed and holy
More, Saviour, like thee."

As to personal appearance Mr. Bliss is thus pictured by one who knew him well:

"He was tall and well-developed in his physical frame, with clustering black hair and a handsome face, possessing easy and polished manners and a very joyous temperament, together with a wealth of sympathy."

Perhaps the most notable traits in Mr. Bliss' character were his "rock-firm God-trust" and his cheerful self-sacrifice.

After the great fire in Chicago he wrote:

"I think God is bringing great good out of this seeming evil. Unite your prayer daily with ours that 'after the fire the still, small voice may be heard and that the Spirit may be poured out in this city."

He wrote a song of comfort to cheer those who had suffered by the fire, and sang it with his grand voice here and there through the city itself and afterwards in a tour with Mr. Moody raising a relief fund. We give two verses of the song below:

"3. Thousands are homeless, and quick to their cry
Heaven-born charity yields a supply,
Upward we glance in our terrible grief,
'Give us this day' brings the promised relief.

"4. Treasures have vanished and riches have flown,
Hopes for the earth-life are blasted and gone,

Courage, O brother, yield not to despair,
'God is our refuge,' his kingdom we share."

Chorus.

" Roll on, roll on, O billow of fire!
Dash with thy fury waves higher and higher
Ours is a mansion abiding and sure,
Ours is a kingdom eternal, secure."

During the sessions of a Sunday-school camp meeting in which he was the musical leader there came up a very sudden and severe gale, rending and throwing to earth the pavilion tent which but an hour previous had been occupied by several hundred persons. Providentially the gale occurred at the noon hour when but few were under it and all these escaped unharmed.

"Is any one killed or hurt?" was Mr. Bliss' first question.

"No."

"Thank God! We must have a praise meeting."

Soon after, at the opening of the afternoon session, with tearful eyes and beaming face he led the great congregation in singing:

" Praise God from whom all blessings flow."

Perhaps the most complete evidence of Mr.

Bliss' trust in God was his actual dependence upon him for daily bread.

In the summer of 1876 a friend congratulated Mrs. Bliss that the immense sale of "Gospel Hymns and Sacred Songs" must have given them at least ten thousand dollars to pay down toward a home. She replied, "Mr. Bliss has not *ten* dollars to pay down on a home. Since January we have been living from day to day, doing the Lord's work with our might and depending upon what he sends us. Although the illness of our children has greatly increased our expenses beyond other years God has sent us enough to supply our needs."

Many are not aware that Mr. Bliss, as well as Mr. Sankey, gave up the royalty upon the "Bliss and Sankey Song Book," (not "The Moody and Sankey Song Book," as it is sometimes thoughtlessly called) and thus sacrificed about thirty thousand dollars, putting the royalty into the hands of Mr. George H. Stuart, Mr. W. E. Dodge, Jr., and Mr. John V. Farwell, to use it for charitable and evangelistic purposes. "Gospel Hymns No. 2," which Mr. Bliss with Mr. Sankey had just completed when he was killed, was sent forth under the same self-sacrificing and benevolent arrangement on the part of the authors.

Mr. Moody recently urged Mr. Bliss to take at least five thousand dollars of the royalty for himself and family, saying that he needed it, but he would not take a dollar. It must all go for the Lord's work.

It was sufficient regard to him thát the songs he had composed were proclaiming the Gospel round the world, being sung not only in Europe, but also in Africa and Asia. I recently heard "Hold the Fort" in Swedish. A missionary letter from Africa reports the singing of it there in the Zulu language, and the Bliss and Sankey collection has also been translated and published (in part) in China, in the native tongue. In India also singing evangelists are using these same hymns.

With the deep God-trust and self-sacrifice Mr. Bliss combined an abounding cheerfulness. His beaming face was a silent psalm assuring the beholder, "Happy is the man that hath the God of Jacob for his help."

He wrote to a friend, "Dr. V—— is jolly,

great and good. Some people are great and good, but can't be jolly. I can't like them quite so well." He wrote out his own heart in that verse of his:

"No darkness have we who in Jesus abide,
The Light of the world is Jesus;
We walk in the light when we follow our guide,
The Light of the world is Jesus."

He has now realized beyond his utmost dreams on earth the heavenly glory and joy of which he sang in another verse of that same hymn as well as in scores of others:

"No need of the sunshine in heaven we're told;
The Light of that world is Jesus.
The Lamb is the light in the City of Gold;
The Light of that world is Jesus."

This sketch would be very incomplete without some record of Mrs. Bliss, whom her husband was pleased to style "My faithful assistant Lou." Mrs. Bliss was herself the composer of several choice pieces of music, both hymns and tunes; one of them a very beautiful tune to the words of "Rock of Ages." She wrote many tunes over the *nom de plume* "*Paulina.*" Whenever circumstances would permit she attended her husband in his public work, aiding him by her voice and by playing accompaniments. It is said that from her he received his first lessons, both in singing and playing. They were indeed of "one accord" in their noble life work. When the sudden summons came she was on the Lord's errand with her husband.

"Lovely and pleasant in their lives, in their deaths they were not divided."

Mr. Bliss leaves a widowed mother of whom he was the only son, and two little ones, Paul and George, aged four and two years. Mr. Moody asks the people of God to take them in charge with their money and their prayers. He himself has raised ten thousand dollars for their support and education, and other free-will offerings have and will come to them from many a Sunday-school where Mr. Bliss' songs are sung, and prayers will rise from many hearts that God will keep them in his sheltering care.

The memorial service in honor of these two Christian workers in Chicago was the largest meeting ever held in that city, showing the loving esteem in which he was held. A monument will be erected to Mr. Bliss' memory, as is most befitting, but the most enduring monument of his life will be "the good he has done," and is still doing by his music and his life, — the monument he so often urged others to raise for themselves, as he sang:

Fading away, like the stars of the morning,
Losing their light in the glorious sun;
So let me steal away, gently and lovingly,
Only remember by what I have done.

So in the harvest, if others may gather
Sheaves from the fields that in spring I have sown;
Who plowed or sowed matters not to the reaper:
I'm only remembered by what I have done.

Fading away like the stars of the morning,
So let my name be unhonored, unknown;
Here, or up yonder, I must be remembered,
Only remembered by what I have done.

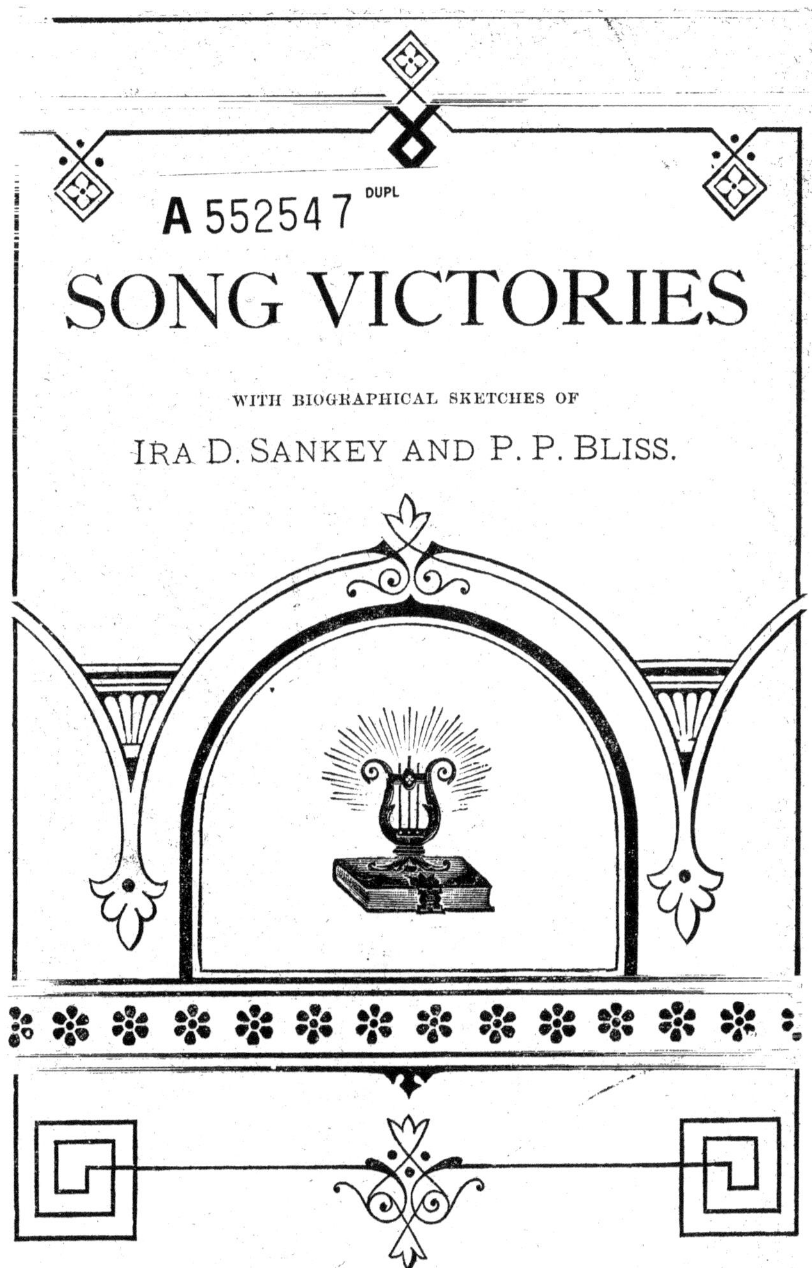

BOSTON: D. LOTHROP & CO., PUBLISHERS.

www.ingramcontent.com/pod-product-compliance
Lightning Source LLC
LaVergne TN
LVHW021401110826
845150LV00007B/1743

* 9 7 8 1 4 2 5 5 1 2 7 5 0 *